Living Awake

The Practice of Transforming Everyday Life

Landon Carter

Living Awake
The Practice of Transforming Everyday Life

Published by CarterCovington
200 Coyote Street #1122, Nevada City, CA 95959

on the Create Space Independent Publishing Platform

Fourth Edition

This book is set in Cambria Type Text.
Printed in the United States of America

First Edition: January 2004
Second Edition: January, 2006
Third Edition: January, 2008
Fourth Edition: January, 2013

Cover and Book Design: Margaret Jean Campbell, ITWGroup.com

Cover photograph is a composite created using an image of the Dart River Valley, New Zealand by Jeff Hitchcock (http://www.flickr.com/photos/arbron/8373450668/) and an image of an eagle by Peter Kaminski (http://www.flickr.com/photos/peterkaminski/3163649535/in/photostream/).

ISBN 13:978-1481976428

ISBN 10:1481976427

ACKNOWLEDGMENTS

There are so many people who have contributed to the insights and information that comprise this book that it is difficult to know where to start and stop. As I sit writing this section, my whole life seems to pass before me surrounded in a mist of gratitude.

First to my parents, George and Peggy Carter, who gave my two brothers and me love and support and a privileged upbringing in rural Minnesota that shaped many of my basic values and beliefs in the goodness of people. My father for his constant love and acceptance of me and the quiet inspiration he has been as a businessman, poet, painter, sportsman and gentleman. My mother for the example she has been in courageously standing up for what she believed, for her unflinching commitment to the environment, for her fight against all forms of racial discrimination, for her love of both animals and humans, and her unbounded energy.

To my brothers, Terry and Bill, for their continuing love and support of their older brother, even when in my arrogance I ignored it. I love you and appreciate who you are.

To the many wonderful women in my life with whom I have had intimate relationships. You have taught me so much of what this book is about. I am only sorry I was such a slow learner that the process took longer and was more painful than it needed to be. If I had only known then what I know now... but that doesn't seem to be the way it works! Thank you.

ACKNOWLEDGEMENTS

To Paramahansa Yogananda for your book Autobiography of a Yogi, which set me on my path.

To Satya Sai Baba, you filled me up with unconditional love when I needed it most, introduced me to a different reality and brought me back to God.

To Indra Devi for teaching me yoga and sharing your home in Tecate, Mexico.

To Werner Erhard for your example and teachings in the realms of Zen and consciousness. I learned my trade from you, brother, both its joys and its pitfalls, and I am grateful. To my fellow trainers in *est* and the staff and volunteers at what is now Landmark Education for the work that you did and still do contributing to the lives of others and for your commitment to transforming the quality of life for people everywhere. Furthermore, the author and publishers wish to thank Landmark Education, LLC, the copyright owner, for the permission to use certain materials originally included in the *est* Training.

To Lazaris and the staff of Concept Synergy for opening up my world to many dimensions, both seen and unseen.

To the staff and trainers at Lifespring for your camaraderie and acceptance of me and the dedication and commitment you have to benefiting others.

To Elise Miller for introducing me to Buddhist meditation practices and the Insight Meditation Society and to Joseph Goldstein and Sharon Salzberg for maintaining the space within which people like me can "know myself."

ACKNOWLEDGEMENTS

To John Thompson and the trainers at Human Factors for bringing together how to make a difference and make money.

To Bob Hoffman, Raz and Liza Ingrasci and the Hoffman Institute (Quadrinity Process) staff for helping me get to issues I wasn't even aware I had and for maintaining the integrity of the deep healing work you do.

To Diamond and River Jamison, Summer Eternity and the rest of the Total Integration Institute for journeys shared and wisdom gained through my participation in "Living Freedom" and your many other events.

To S. N. Goenka and the volunteers at the Dhamma Vipassana Meditation Centre in New Zealand for teaching me the Buddha's path for eliminating suffering and for the opportunity to deeply explore my inner nature while being supported and cared for.

To my many friends who have stood by me through the ups and downs of my life and whose advice, council and most of all friendship I deeply cherish: Steve Pomerance and Allyn Feinberg, Myron and Sharon Wick, Don and Jean Altshuler, Joe and Helen Bouscaren, Christina Campbell, Mac and Peny Carter, Bente Haubro Carter, Jane Downes, Stewart and Joanie Emery, Bill Erkelens and Marie Roehm, Summer Eternity, Tony Freedley and Barbara Holmes, Al and Cristi Guenter, Malcolm Gefter and Kathy Kirk, Duncan and Gail Howat, Duffy and Tricia Herman, Ned Hoke, Kelly Kamin, Linda Kennett, Jimmy and Sue II Knownes, Nancy Knowles, Randy Kunkle, Edgar Kaiser, Peter Lenn, Tom and Flame Lutes, Tallo and Beatrice Masias,

ACKNOWLEDGEMENTS

Bruce and Jean McHardy, Jeffrey Mironov and Brenda Charles, Sally Ann Ranney, Allan and Alisha Ridgen, Tracy Rivkin, Bob Rout, Cherie Carter-Scott and Michael Pomeje, Lawrence and Sunni Stoller, Frank Sloan and Catherine Martin, Patrick Sullivan, Victoria Saunders, Sika and Caitlin, Joshua and Meike Sullivan, Dick and Flo Tonks, Beky Townsend, Jack Zwizzig.

And finally, to my three wonderful and brilliant children, Eden, Erinn and Bryn. You have given me the honor of participating with you while you grew up and through loving you I have learned much about love.

CONTENTS

Forward to First Edition

My original purpose for writing this book was to share with my children what I have learned in the thirty-some years since I first woke up to myself and started to seek answers to life's many mysteries. While the three of them were growing up, I never felt I had the complete conversation about what Dad thinks about life, so this is my gift to them. However, as I began teaching this material in seminars recently and started to see the results in the participants' lives, I realized I wanted to make this material more broadly available. I therefore expanded my purpose to include sharing what I have learned with you, the reader.

The intent of this book is to take you through an enlightening process of gaining insights into who you are and the nature of the reality in which you find yourself. These insights, plus the techniques presented, will allow you to experience more freedom in areas of your life previously constricted and constrained and will empower you to be able to create more happiness, love and fulfillment in the very place where it counts the most—your everyday life.

I grew up in a small mid-western farm town riding horses, playing sports, becoming an Eagle Scout, and working on the neighbor's farm. I had supportive, loving parents who took my two younger brothers and me skiing in Colorado and camping in the summers. While we all had household chores we complained about, we had a fairly privileged upbringing and were never in real want. At fifteen, I was sent off to some of the best schools America has to offer: Andover, Yale and Harvard Business School. At school, I worked hard to get better than average academic scores and make the first team varsity in American football, skiing, lacrosse and later rugby.

At 23 I married the sister of my Andover roommate, thus fulfilling a decision I had made to marry her, when I was fifteen and she was eleven. After I graduated with an MBA from Harvard, she and I went to Peru for two years in the Peace Corps. At this point everything had pretty much worked out for Bunky (my nickname) Carter. I had done everything right: doing well at the best schools, marrying the right girl, and excelling at sports. My expectation was that after the struggle of finally getting to adulthood, I would now ride off into the sunset to a happy life.

While in the Peace Corps in Peru, my wife left me (there was just so much of "me" in my life that there was hardly any room for her) and the fantasy bubble burst. Suddenly things were falling apart and I wasn't sure how to make my life work anymore. I returned from the Peace Corps to live and work in Aspen, Colorado, and over the next two years, while working on the development of Snowmass Resort, I put together many of the elements of the American dream of success. I had a condominium two blocks from the ski lift, a girlfriend or two, money in the bank, a motocross bike in the garage, and the job I wanted. But I wasn't happy. I thought, "If I'm not happy now, what about when I'm forty and have three times all this stuff; how am I going to be happy then?" There just seemed to be something missing, some piece of the puzzle I hadn't gotten while growing up.

As an aside, I have observed that in order to wake up, most people require a catalytic experience. Some people "bottom out", whereby most aspects of their lives are not working and they finally realize they have a great deal to do with the mess. Some others, like me, "top out", whereby they have everything yet still feel an emptiness, a sense of betrayal of some unspoken promise, and experience confusion, depression and unhappiness.

A few sessions at the local therapist's office didn't seem to help. Then I read Autobiography of a Yogi by Paramahansa Yogananda. This landmark book opened up a whole new world of possibility for me and started me meditating, eating vegetarian food, and thinking outside the western scientific model of "how things are" within which I had grown up and unquestioningly operated in since birth.

I next heard about Satya Sai Baba, read some of his translated talks, and felt drawn to go to India to see this miracle worker with my own eyes. I asked myself, "If I had been a Roman soldier at the time of Christ, would I have walked over the hills to see Him, or would I have complacently ordered another beer?" So off I went to India, where over the next seven months I was introduced to a very different reality and, for the first time in my adult life, felt filled up with love and acceptance.

In India, one experience in particular had a profound effect on me. A man who had been attending Sai Baba's discourses for months was crippled by arthritis to such an extent that he had to be carried on a stretcher, yet he was always happy and grateful to be in India in Baba's presence. One day he was carried into Baba's house for a private interview and walked out about five minutes later, completely healed! I was so moved by the miracle of that event and the love that Sai Baba had shown this man that I cried for an hour over the pettiness and pretense of my little life and then and there committed myself to helping others if I could.

My path since that trip to India in 1972 has been a conscious effort to know myself and to learn how to consciously take charge of my life and be happy. I have had some great teachers along the way: some who were formally in that role, but many disguised as my female partners or even as the students in my seminars. I have made many mistakes and at different times both failed as well as succeeded in most arenas of my life.

This book comes out of my own experience and from what I have found to be useful to the 70,000 people I have had the privilege of working with over the years. It is often said, "We teach what we most need to learn ourselves." This has certainly been true for me as I deepened my understanding of this material through the many repetitions of teaching it, and the material gradually permeated my own life.

The intent of this book is to empower you to BE more of who you want to be, to DO more of what you want to do, and to HAVE more of what you want to have. There are no guarantees, of course, that this material will benefit you as each of us seems to be on our own path. I only know about mine and some of what others have shared about theirs. However, from what others have told me of their lives I believe the information is relatively universal and that this book can be of great assistance to you in creating more love, happiness and peace in your life.*

For those of you who are just starting to examine metaphysical questions, the book presents a comprehensive map or model of who we are in our reality. A good map/model will help you negotiate your life more efficiently on the road to what you want. But please remember, just as a word or label is not the thing itself, a map is not the true territory, but only an approximation of the way it is.

Some models, however, have allowed for great human progress. An example of this is Isaac Newton's physics, which was used to get a man to the moon even when it was already known to not be the complete answer (the model of general relativity replaced it). So in that vein, the models presented in this book will give you an empowering approach to the questions of how to create more of what you want.

For those of you who have consciously been on your path for a long time, these models should remind you of what you know, perhaps fill in a gap or two, and give you a way of integrating what you know into a useful process.

*The BE-DO-HAVE conversation was originally included in the *est* Training and is reprinted with the permission of Landmark Education, LLC. All rights reserved.

I will start to answer the question "Who am I?" by presenting various models that hone in on useful understandings about beingness and the mind. These models include: *Who am I and what is the ego; how the reptilian brain functions; the structure and functioning of the mind; how your personality is formed; and how reality is created through your perceptive mechanism.* Then I will present *the core consideration* which became the underlying premise of the reality in which you now find yourself as well as the prime motivation for your personality. After a brief discussion of the nature of reality, we will look at *the fundamental choice* necessary to empower yourself.

With that as a foundation, I will present a process, *The Seven Steps of Transformation,* for enacting fundamental change in your life. When followed, this process is designed to take you from where you are to where you want to be.

The remainder of the book will discuss the application of these understandings to creating a positive reality, to having successful relationships, and to dealing with worry, boredom and other common experiences, which seem to rob us of our happiness.

I would like to make one last point by way of introduction. YOU DON'T NEED TO DO ANY OF THIS. If you can simply stay present and awake to yourself in this moment of now, you can create all of what you would ever want. For isn't it true that in this moment, right now, whatever is **actually** happening in your life is **now** happening and whatever changes you were going to make, can only really be made in a moment of now, just like this moment? So to be constantly awake to each moment would mean dealing with your life through the only window you have ever had available to you—Right Now.

The problem seems to be the incredible power of our unconscious mind to put us back to sleep, so that not only do we miss the moment, but we are also lulled either into a false promise that sometime in the future it is all going to work out, or the equally false despair that it's never going to work out. To break the grip of my unconscious mind has been my 30-plus year struggle; and it has been in this struggle that the usefulness of the models and processes presented in this book have proven themselves.

I consider myself to be somewhat of a metaphysical slug in that my steps have been slow, small, and through the mud, and often the lessons have had to be repeated a number of times before I learned them. I have had no major revelations out of which this material has been written, which means if I can understand it and make it work for me, then so can you. I also make no claims to be other than simply another person on his path, sharing with you what I have found and looking forward to what is next. May we all be happy and wise.

Forward to Second Edition

Since publishing the first edition of this book, I have been learning about and experimenting in my own life with the process of creating reality. During this time, I have been strongly influenced by the Abraham material as presented by Esther and Jerry Hicks, especially their book "Ask and It Is Given." This material can be summarized under the general heading of "the law of attraction" which states "like attracts like." In other words, if you vibrate at a certain frequency, in part symbolized by your emotional state, are clear about what you desire, and if your belief structure will "allow" it to happen, you will attract to you what you desire.

As a result, I recognized that the material of my book heavily emphasizes the process of getting rid of programming and patterning from the past in order to make space for creating something new. I still concur with all I have written, but I feel I need to rebalance the material so that more importance is given to getting clear about what you want and then knowing the methodology for bringing it about in your life. To accomplish this, I have added comments to the end of Chapter Four.

One important caveat is that often what we want from one conscious state of mind is not really what we want from another—shall we say, "higher" or "more freed up" state of consciousness. The classic example is someone who wants lots of money, gets it and then discovers it isn't what they wanted because it didn't solve their original dissatisfaction. Sometimes this only becomes knowable through the experience of getting what you desire. On the other hand if you suspect that what you desire may not give you the experience you are looking for or, as in my case, you can't figure out what you do want, then focus on your known patterns, looking deeply into the assumptions, thoughts and emotions that comprise these patterns and letting them go. This will create space and new states of awareness will arise and with them new and different desires. And so it seems to go in a spiral of ascending stages of consciousness, each with it's new desires, followed by desire fulfillment, with the accompanying new experiences, followed by a new stage of consciousness, ad infinitum!

At the same time there can be an increasing sense of detachment for the world of "havingness", and accompanying sense of inner peace, and a growing experience of the existence of "who you are" beyond time, space and form. May this mysterious adventure of life bring you joy.

FORWARD TO FOURTH EDITION

I recently married Diane Covington, a writer, who first contacted me with some suggestions to improve this book. It has taken me three years to implement her suggestions! In the meantime we have written a book together called *Falling in Love Backwards: an unlikely tale of Happily Ever After* that validates in our lives what I had written about in this book. *Falling in Love Backwards* is not only a good romance story but also a "how to" book on relationships that requires an understanding of the concepts presented here in *Living Awake.*

As we worked through the many issues that we each brought to the relationship, the models and concepts from this book proved themselves over and over again as we released old dysfunctional patterns and experienced more and more freedom and connection. This deepening experience of love has taken us to realms of ecstasy and pleasure we didn't know existed and brought up some of our deepest insecurities and fears to be healed. It is therefore without reservation that I recommend the methodology and practices of this book for anyone wanting freedom from the bondage of the ego/mind and the unhappiness it produces in one's life.

May we all regain the wonder of childhood for the ongoing adventure of life.

How to Use this Book

I have written this book as a dialogue between you and me. I intend it to be challenging and penetrating. It is also designed to stimulate a personal process of deep introspection into the very nature of your being and how you function. I suggest that you read the book in order, front to back, so as to understand the vocabulary and references and therefore have the foundation for the next section. From time to time there will be exercises. I strongly urge you to do these at the time of your first reading so that you will have the personal experience to validate the concepts that follow. You will need a **notebook** in which to do these exercises and record your personal experiences and insights.

My suggestion is to sit with each section of material without trying to assess whether what I have said is universally true or not. Rather take the view of asking, "What within my direct experience validates this point?" thereby trying the model on, so to speak. Again, please don't take any one model as "the truth", yet attempt to find the truth of the model in your own experience. It is only by making this material alive in your personal experience that it becomes of real value. Whatever

I write can only at best create an opening for insights about yourself, but can never be the truth in and of itself.

Of course you can read right through the book, but to really get the value that is available, I would suggest you plan to spend several weeks on this material. First, read and re-read each section to make sure you really understand it. Notice what is coming up for you as you read each section and then in the weeks to follow. Have your pen and notebook by your side when you read so you can take notes on your own insights and/or personal experiences that validate the material. Finally do each exercise in your notebook using the estimated time as a guide. Another powerful way to go through this material is with a friend, helping each other with the exercises and sharing your insights. I especially recommend this for couples.

My starting premise and ending point is that each of us is creating our own reality. I believe I can demonstrate this to you in your own experience if you will follow along with each model as the complete argument unfolds. At times there will be points which appear extraneous to the main thread of the argument; hopefully you will see how they all fit together by the end. Each of the models, tools and techniques I am presenting has been very useful to me in my own evolution and, by their own admission, useful to the many thousands of people with whom I have had the privilege of working over the years as seminar leader and coach.

CHAPTER ONE

Who Am I?

Rather than argue with the many theological models attempting to answer the question, "Who am I?" I ask that you simply turn to your own internal experience. Sometimes closing your eyes helps to break the fascination with the outside world, so after reading each statement close your eyes for a moment to reflect on whether what you are reading is true for you. Internally you can experience many sensations inside your body. Stop, close your eyes, and be aware of some of your body sensations.

You can also notice and identify your emotions. Stop again to notice how you feel right now. You can observe your thoughts, the chatter inside your head, which might even now be saying, "What's he talking about?"--- that voice that keeps you company! Stop and notice your internal dialogue. You also can be aware when you are experiencing images from the past (remembering) or imagining possible events in the future (planning, expecting or worrying). Add to that list a certain set of labels, beliefs, preferences, and behaviors, all self-observable by the way, and you have what most of us would call "Me."

During my initial trip to India in 1972 to see Satya Sai Baba, I visited the ashram of Ramana Maharshi in Tiruvannamalai near Mount Arunachala. It was said that Ramana Maharshi went into a tomb, lay down and imagined himself dying. By completely letting go of everything he considered himself to be, he became a fully self-realized being. Subsequently he taught people the powerful meditative technique of self-inquiry. The instructions are to ask yourself the question, "Who am I?" and sit quietly to observe what your mind brings up in response to that question. Then explore the true nature of what your mind has latched onto in answering that round of inquiry so as to be able to say, "Not that, not that." This could go on for days until you are left without another answer and a momentary cessation of the mind chatter—the experience of simply being present in the Here and Now.

One day I was sitting in a large group of hundreds of Sai Baba devotees, silently meditating on, "Who am I?" while I waited for him to appear. There was no instruction from Baba to do this meditation; it was just something I had decided to do on my own. When Sai Baba passed me on the way to giving his afternoon's discourse, he stopped, and with a twinkle in his eye laughingly asked me, "Yes, who are you?" Letting the laughter subside, he proceeded on his way. I had said nothing during the entire time, so I was needless to say shocked by his ability to read my exact thoughts!

Exercise 1

"Who am I?"

(40 minutes to one hour)

Take out your notebook and write the question "Who am I?" at the top of a page. Now close your eyes if you need to and ask yourself, or have a friend ask you, the question, "Who am I?" Write down whatever comes to you in response to the question. Take whatever your mind brings up as you ask yourself the question over and over again and write it down on your list. Try not to monitor or analyze your response at this point—just record what your mind brings up. Do this until there are no new answers.

Now go through your list and identify what on the list is something that you <u>have</u> and put an "H" beside those items (examples: PhD, "I am rich" = have money in the bank, "husband" = have a wife, "father" = have children). Go through the list again and identify all the items that are what you <u>do</u> and put a "D" beside those items (examples: "a cook" = do cooking, "a good Samaritan" = do good deeds, "a sailor" = do sailing). What remains on the list will be *who you consider yourself to be* and you can put a "B" beside those items.

Your list might include your name or a title you have, male or female (body you have), father or mother, artist, brother, spendthrift (the way you 'do' money), loving person, grew up poor (history you have), average student (self image you have), a black American (skin color you have, place you were born), president of bowling club, a golfer, a Christian (beliefs you have), Jew or Hindu, etc.

Now go through the list item by item and see if that item is really you, the essence of you. For example: I am a husband, which means I <u>have</u> a wife, and since I am obviously not my wife I must take her out of the equation of who I am by eliminating her from the list. Put a check mark beside each item you can honestly say, "That is not who I am." Then there are the things a husband does like going to work and bringing home money and sleeping with a wife and fathering children. Look at these items and ask yourself, "Am I still me if I were to stop doing all those activities?" If the answer is "Yes" then you can eliminate all those activities since once again they are not essentially who you are.

Continue through the list to see how many of the items you can eliminate by actually examining their true nature in relation to who you actually are. If you cut off your arm or leg wouldn't you still be you? Isn't your body a bunch of atoms with a huge amount of space between them? Are you the atoms or the space? If you changed your religion or your beliefs wouldn't you still be you? Are you what you have, whether it be belief or thought or emotion or some physical thing?

Keep examining these questions until you get a deep sense of your own knowing about these questions. Are you what you do? And finally; Are you what you consider yourself to be? Isn't the nature of a consideration, a thought or concept you have?

Which brings us full circle once again to the question, "Who are you?" So much of what we seem so attached to and defend so vigorously may be nothing but an illusion!

While it is true that teenagers sometimes think they are their car or hair or clothes, as adults we certainly know that if we wreck the car, cut the hair or change the clothes, we still exist. However, most of us, even as adults, are very attached to and identified with our labels, which we consider ourselves to be (reference your long list from Exercise 1). It is equally true that anything you can observe, notice, or be aware of can't really be you. Or at least, when you have accounted for everything you call "yourself", there still remains outside that list or set, **The**

Watcher/ Observer Self—that which is noticing. The better question might be, "Who is watching? Who is observing?" The experience of being the observer is closer to who you really are than any of the things from your list that are constantly changing or subject to change. Notice that The Observer is formless and always in the Here and Now. Regardless of what changes on your list, The Observer is always simply Being Here Now.

> Go back to your list now and from the perspective of The Observer, see if you can eliminate any more Have's, Do's, or Be's.

The experience of Enlightenment, of being awake to yourself, is nothing more than being aware that you are being aware of yourself in the present moment. While this experience is always available to us, for the most part we are so conditioned and in fact lost in ourselves and our reality that we are not awake to ourselves. Many spiritual disciplines offer techniques to help you keep in touch with yourself as The Observer. One is to notice your in-breath and out-breath, either at the nostrils or at the diaphragm, and another is to feel sensations in your body. Both of these bring you into the present moment where whatever is happening in your life is actually taking place and can be experienced.

The *"who you consider yourself to be"* is normally called the ego. It would appear that a portion of our consciousness, the portion that is able to observe and make choices, is perpetually lost in our egos. Therefore we go through life subjected only to what the ego is able to produce and limited by its past conditioning. It is as if we, the actor, took on a role early in life, played it over and over again until we learned it by heart and then somewhere in the process forgot that we are actors. Now lost to who we really are, we consider ourselves to be only the role.

Some of what the role includes may still work for you. Unfortunately other aspects may not. These need to be released and replaced by more workable attitudes, beliefs, and behaviors. The process of releasing and replacing requires being awake to yourself. In addition to being awake, the freedom to choose what will work in any given situation is a function of being able to be in the Now in a non-attached way. This book will assist you in that process.

AWAKEN THE OBSERVER SELF

The essential skill necessary for the work of transformation is to be able to be "awake to yourself," to keep the Observer's consciousness present. The Buddhists call this "mindfulness." I will refer to it as "**keeping your watcher on**" or "**being The Observer.**"

Most of us tend to look out at the world, noticing and focusing on things from the plane of our eyes outward. In order to be awake to yourself, you need to move the plane of your observation to just behind your head, so that you include what is going on inside your own experience in the observation. What you will then notice can be described as a hierarchy in the nature of how things are occurring. At the same time, you will be experiencing the natural flow of how we actually create reality, from the most ethereal to the most physically solid.

The hierarchy is:

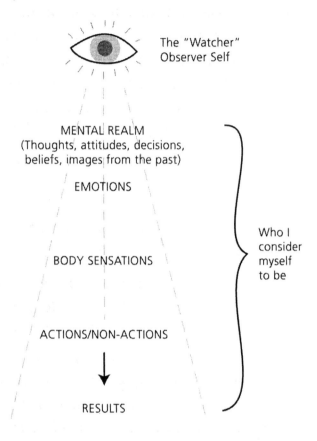

Instead of seeing only the results and wondering "Why is the world around me showing up the way it is?" you will start to see that your actions as well as your non-actions (like allowing things to happen without doing anything about them) have a direct relationship to the results in your life. This includes things like your wealth, health, and how people relate to you. Then you will start to see that your emotions drive your actions, whether it is a strong desire for something that motivates you to go out and get it, or avoidance of something you fear or hate.

Out of anger may come punishing behaviors or, if suppressed, covert actions and depression. You might notice that you always do what you really feel like doing and justify it with a lot of reasons. And on a deeper level, you will start to notice that emotions are the body's reaction to your mental state. They actually arise out of some deep-seated mental beliefs about yourself and the way you experience the world. Still deeper, you might notice that you are actually reacting to physical sensations in your body that you either dislike and want to get rid of/avoid, or that you like and want to retain/have. All of these levels of your internal experience and relationships between them can be observed when you stay awake to yourself.

Once you start to see the causal nature of the different aspects of yourself, you gain additional choices further up the hierarchy in a more ethereal realm, if you will, and before the results become so solid that only damage control remains. In the 1980s when I was attending Concept Synergy lectures, the presenter, Lazaris, used to say, "If you can listen to the whispers, you don't have to hear the screams." For example, if someone says something and you automatically react in anger, you get whatever mess that angry response creates in your life.

Instead, suppose you observe the anger arising in you. By being in touch with your body sensations where the anger first manifests, you would then be able to stop the automatic response, thus not automatically creating the same old result. Now, by being able to take a more appropriate action from a position of choice, perhaps you will create a more desirable result. As you observe your anger further, you might start to see how your anger comes from a certain mental attitude or belief and that if you changed that attitude or belief you would not be angry in a similar situation.

By way of example, suppose your fundamental belief about yourself is, "I am not good enough." It would be fairly easy for someone through their comments or criticism to trigger a hurt response in you. Underneath most anger is hurt, but without observing what is actually happening you might only feel the anger rising up in your body, then blame the other for causing it, and want to punish him for his unkind words. If, in the course of observing your anger, you saw the hurt behind the anger and were able to see the belief about yourself underneath the hurt; and if you were able to change that belief to one of "I am enough, whole and complete", then it would be true that, "Sticks and stones will break my bones but words will never hurt me."

Until you change that fundamental belief, however, words do hurt! The old adage, "No one can make you feel badly about yourself except yourself" becomes true only when you can observe the true nature of how your own mechanism works. But once again, without being aware and awake to yourself in these challenging situations, your conditioned responses control you, rather than you being able to observe your response, let it be, and not react.

To be able to observe yourself in the midst of different situations takes practice. You must gradually build your skill to stay centered and present. This is why many eastern religions talk about practices. Just like going to a gym to get stronger by lifting smaller then larger weights, these practices have methodologies that lead to mastery of this skill.

MEDITATION PRACTICE

A major component of being able to stay awake to yourself is the ability to concentrate: to focus your attention and keep it focused on one thing. This is why the first step of meditation practice is really one of concentration. The easiest and most straightforward method is the concentration on your breath as it passes in and out of your nostrils. You will notice that the breath changes according to your different experiences: if you are calm, the breath will be likewise, and if you are agitated, so will the breath be. So not only is the practice of following your breath good for concentration, but it is also a great way of bringing you into the present moment and starting to give you an indication of what's going on inside your experience.

When you first start this practice, it is astonishing to realize that almost any thought which arises will carry you off into its fantasy land, be it memory or future projection. Over time, you will find that your power of concentration will grow so that the thoughts and images drift in and out of your awareness while you stay present, observing your breath.

EXERCISE 2

Developing your Observer Presence

(20 minutes)

Sit in a relaxed but upright position. Close your eyes and notice your breath coming in and out at the end of your nostrils. Start by counting, "One, two, three,...."

with each in-breath. Do this until you get to ten, then start at one again. If at any time you get lost, forget where you are, or get carried away with an image, go back to "One" again. Do this until you can do the exercise for 10 minutes in a relaxed way without missing a beat.

At this point if you feel you can stay present without getting distracted by your own thoughts, drop the counting and simply stay with the in and out breath. If you start being too distracted or find your mind quite agitated, use the counting again. Make this a 20-minute daily meditation practice.

The skill you attain through this meditation practice will contribute greatly to your ability to stay centered in yourself and aware of yourself throughout the remainder of the day. Think of how difficult it is to stay present with your breath when your eyes are closed and merely a thought can carry you off. Imagine just how much more difficult it is to stay awake, remaining in the Observer Self consciousness, when your eyes are open and the whole world is demanding your attention.

So this is something you work on at first in a quiet place with few distractions. As the skill increases, you will be able to sustain that awakened consciousness in more demanding circumstances. Only from this non-place place of observation is there any real choice in your life, all else being automatic as it comes from the conditioned mind.

This does not make the conditioned mind bad. Nor am I saying that some of the things arising from automatic thinking, conditioned decision making, reactive emotions, and mechanical behaviors are not desirable. But be aware that if there is no conscious choice involved, then there is no ability to change to a more desired result if what keeps showing up is not what you want. Only by staying awake to yourself will you have conscious choice.

CHAPTER TWO

Our Human Mechanisms

We are multi-dimensional beings, with the ability to be aware of our physical, emotional and mental dimensions. But for the most part we don't know how this organism that we seem so attached to and so trapped in, operates. The next sections describe certain operating functions of our human mechanism and how these functions influence our life experience. We will look at the relationship between fear and risk and how this relationship plays out in our daily interactions. We will also look at a useful model of the survival mind, at how perception determines the extent of our awareness, and finally, at an important choice between being responsible or being a victim.

Many of these models or versions of them were first introduced to me when I was working as a trainer for various human potential/enlightenment organizations: first with *est* (now Landmark Education) in the 70's, then Lifespring in the late 80's, and finally Human Factors in the 90's. I owe a great deal to my teachers: Werner Erhard and the *est* trainer body, John Hanley and the Lifespring staff, and John Thompson and the trainer/consultants at Human Factors. The members of these organizations were committed to doing what worked in producing results in people's lives.

It was during this time in my life that I learned to surrender to what worked and give up what didn't. As each of the founders ran a business, there were very definite measurements in terms of the number of people signing up for future courses, the number of interested guests brought to events, and other customer satisfaction statistics that were indicators of the value participants received from the seminars. If it worked they would keep it; if it didn't they would throw it out.

After my time in India, where so much of what I was introduced to was based on a cosmology I didn't understand or experience, I was pleased that I could pursue enlightenment in a very practical way consistent with my Yale engineering background and Harvard Business School education. The following models have met the test of practical workability over the years.

The Role of Fear: The Reptile Within

Many spiritual books have said that we are either operating out of fear or love. While I agree, I think it is too simple an explanation without a very clear understanding of how fear actually operates in our lives.

General Adaptation Syndrome

(15 minutes)

To help you follow this explanation experientially, recall a time or a situation in which you experienced a great deal of fear. Perhaps it was being in a very high place, or a time when you had to make a public presentation, or just some other scary experience. Now observe all the physical sensations in your body and behaviors that you did or didn't do. In your notebook, make a list of what fear feels like as it manifests in your body. This list is now your version of what is called the ***general adaptation syndrome.***

This list will probably include some of the following of what is called the sympathetic nervous system's general adaptation response: increased heart rate, increased mental activity including questions like, "What do I do? How do I get out of this?"; a heightened sense of awareness, sweaty palms and underarms, cold extremities, tension in the thighs, perhaps even heat, a narrowing of vision, dry mouth, tension or fluttering in the abdomen ("butterflies in the stomach"), feeling sick in your stomach, feeling the need to defecate or urinate, paralysis, constriction of the chest, and various other tensions, aches and pains around the body. These are more or less intense, depending on how afraid you are.

If your task was to get up in front of others to make a public presentation, almost none of the above physical, emotional, and mental responses helped you get the job done. In fact, most of us experience them as hindrances, the experience of fear we wish we didn't have. And it is not as if you said to yourself "Gee, I'm going to give a speech, I think a little dry mouth will help!" If, on the other hand, a saber-tooth tiger was about to attack, more of the symptoms would certainly be beneficial as automatic responses preparing you to fight or run away so as to survive.

Certain systems are being turned on to high gear: heart rate, mental activity, heightened awareness and blood flow to the large muscles of your thighs and shoulders. At the same time, certain systems are being shut down: the eating and eliminating system, the blood to the extremities (sweat cools as the blood vessels constrict), plus a coagulant is being pumped into the blood in case of injury. These responses occur automatically and precognitively (meaning before we normally become consciously aware of the response).

The problem arises when this automatic system is used to respond to so many different situations, especially in an environment of few saber-tooth tigers and many public presentations!

Two of my most noticeable fears were a general fear of what other people would think of me and a fear of heights. In my early twenties I would get sweaty palms and underarms just walking into a restaurant. The trip between the door to sitting at the table was anything but pleasant. Also at about that time, I started rock climbing with the Yale Mountaineering Club. I would climb to prove what a hero I was, putting together in my mind the great story of my accomplishments, all the while being terrified during the experience itself. It was only after I learned from Werner Erhard how to observe my fear during my days as an *est* trainer in my 30's, that I was able to overcome these fears and actually start enjoying the experience of climbing and being up in front of other people.

We have a triune, or three-part brain: reptilian brain (the reticular formation), limbic brain and the neo-cortex.

TRIUNE BRAIN

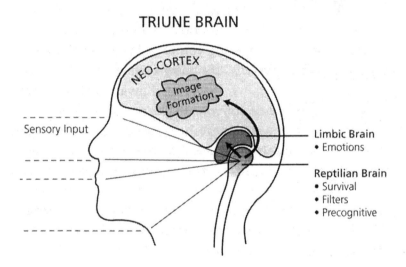

From an evolutionary point of view these brains seem to have been additive. In other words, as species became more complex, necessary functions were accomplished by a new brain added to the old. The smallest and simplest part is the reptilian brain into which the sensory signals from all sensory receptors first go. Everything picked up by our five senses (sights, sounds, smells, tactile pressures, and tastes) first goes to the reptilian brain, which checks precognitively whether a threat to survival exists. This survival function can afford to make many mistakes on the false alarm (false negative) side of the equation.

It can afford no mistakes on the "a threat was really there but it didn't appear as one" (false positive) side. Therefore, the reptilian brain functions as if everything that reminds it of a previous threat is a threat and anything that **reminds** it of one of those reminders is also a threat. It is kind of an "Everything is the same as everything else, except not always" algorithm. If you watch a lizard, and a cloud comes between it and the sun, the lizard goes into its fight/flight/freeze mode. After all, it might have been the early warning of a hawk looking for dinner.

Even with the lack of saber-tooth tigers, it might not be too bad to live with such an automatic and non-discriminatory system, but there seems to be one more caveat to the reptilian brain's modus operandi. This involves how the reptilian brain carries out its survival-focused duties. The purpose of the reptilian brain is "To cause the survival of the entity (so far so good) or anything the entity considers itself to be." The last part of that statement is where most of the trouble originates.

We as Beings consider ourselves to be not just our bodies, but also our ideas, our history, our point of view about this and that, how we feel about things, what we think others think about us (our reputation), our membership in group or country, and any other concepts with which we identify—usually preceded by "my or mine." This means that the reptilian brain and the entire system it conjures up is now dedicated to the survival of who you consider yourself to be: your EGO.

When you stand up to make a public presentation, your body certainly isn't in much danger, especially since most audiences stopped throwing tomatoes some time ago. But your ego is threatened in that the audience might reject your ideas, or disapprove of your performance and that to the ego means rejecting you and, as we shall see later, that triggers some of your worst fears. Thus the whole mechanism of the reptilian brain comes into play and your body reacts at a physical level, whether it is useful or not.

EVERYDAY FEAR

If we now look at how the mechanism of fight/flight/freeze plays out in everyday communication and everyday actions, it is easy to observe that the simple exchange of ideas is most often not an exchange at all. Instead it is an attempt to win your point at the expense of the other losing his or hers, to make yourself right and the other wrong, or to justify (and thus be right about) your view and your actions while invalidating others. In addition your ego survives by taking over situations: it must dominate and control or try to avoid being dominated or controlled. In all these ways the ego—my ideas, my view, my religion, my, my, my......... survives. To the extent a person is convinced that his survival is somehow tied to the survival of an idea (like my religion or my country), you will even see people give up their lives to defend the idea, thus the expression "dead right." This does not just go on at the level of wars. How many times have you seen people give up their aliveness, the love and happiness in their lives, to be right about some point of view or other?

EXERCISE 4

The Right/Wrong Game

(40 minutes)

Recall an incident in which you found yourself arguing with another. In your notebook write how you were right about your view and made the other wrong. How you justified your stance and invalidated the other's. How you won and they lost, or if you lost, how you justified it. Now record your emotional experience of that incident and how you think it was for the other person. Also, as a result of that interaction did you experience more affinity or more distance?

Recall another incident in which you ended up taking over control of a situation or avoided being controlled by someone else. What was your internal experience? How did it end up on an affinity/distancing scale?

Recall other instances, listing your strategy for being right and the cost to you both internally in your own experience and externally in your relations with others.

Make a list of your most prevalent right and/or wrong behaviors.

You would think that intelligent people like us could see through this charade, but the fear response mechanism is precognitive and therefore automatic unless you are very awake to yourself and your own automatic stimulus-response mechanism. In addition, the need to be right, to win, to justify, to control and dominate or avoid being dominated is pervasive in our culture and therefore a big part of our early conditioning.*

Underneath these dysfunctional behaviors and the need to be right, is fear. Given that emotions supply the energy for and drive your behaviors, it would seem essential to know when fear was present. This would allow a choice as to how you wanted to respond to create your desired results. However, most people are almost totally out of touch with their emotions, be they fear, sadness, anger or even joy, except when these feelings have built up to such an extent that they literally explode in an emotional outburst. Why is this? One explanation is that most of us grew up in families and in a culture where it was not OK to express emotions, so we learned to suppress them and not pay attention to them. Emotions are too wild, too scary, too out of control, and certainly not rational. The problem is that the emotions then run your actions without you being aware that they are doing so and therefore without the choice which would have been possible had you been aware.

Again, this is the reason to do your quiet sitting practice so as to build the concentration necessary to observe and experience what is going on as it is occurring. Only then do you have a choice to do something different from what you have

---

*The conversations about the right/wrong game and the structure of the mind were originally included in the *est* Training and are reprinted with the permission of Landmark Education, LLC. All rights reserved.

always done before. Insanity could be defined as doing the same thing over and over again hoping for a different result—and none of us would consciously act in this insane way if we saw we had a choice. Being awake to yourself is not only your greatest tool for transformation; it is the foundation for creating a new reality. So keep practicing.

THE MIND

I will next present a useful model for the mind, which explains how the mind operates in furthering the survival of the ego. This model, designated "Anatomy of the Mind", was originally included in the *est* Training and is reprinted with the permission of Landmark Education LLC. All rights reserved.

First, what is the mind? The mind is a stack of multi-sensory holographic records of successive moments of now. Each multi-sensory holographic record is an exact and total replica of the three-dimensional reality in which we live, including all our body sensations, sensory input, emotions, thoughts, what we saw, sensed, and how we felt about it. You experience them as memories. This is why if I mention "burnt toast," you will probably remember not only the smell, but also perhaps an image associated with that smell of you being in your family kitchen as a child.

The sense of time comes about through the ordered nature of the stack of images, and the fact that you can access them gives you the sense of having a past. What you notice when you really look is that there is this great moment of NOW, and that the existence of the stack of images in this Here and Now gives the illusion of time and a past.

What is the purpose of the mind? The purpose of the mind is the survival of the being or anything the being considers itself to be. Who you consider yourself to be is your ego, in which case the mind's entire function is to cause your ego to survive.

How does it do this? There are certain types of incidents in your past that the mind considered important to note. These are incidents involving situations where survival was apparently threatened and you survived by doing whatever you happened to do at the time. Whether what you did actually contributed to your survival is not important as the mind now links those actions with your being able to survive in similar situations in the future.

There are three types of these incidents that the mind registers important to survival. From most important to least important, they are: (A) core incidents containing physical trauma and pain, some degree of unconsciousness, and of course threat to survival; (B) secondary incidents containing emotional trauma in which you felt victimized and had some kind of loss accompanied by strong emotions; and (C) tertiary incidents we know as "upsets" which are replayed reminders of the earlier other two.

These incidents are strung together through similarities into what we know as "patterns of behavior" that include physical sensations, emotions, thoughts, your thinking process, behaviors, and so on. When replayed in some current moment, the new incident with all its details gets recorded as another (C) upset and is added to the string of similar incidents that make up this particular "pattern of behavior". The intermittent replaying of this pattern - being upset again - reinforces the pattern and keeps it alive.

The Mind: A Stack of Images

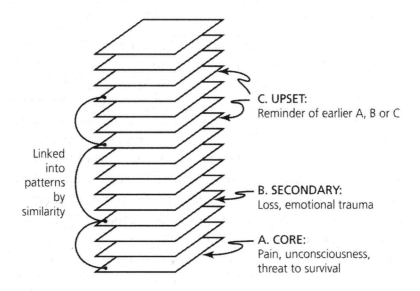

Linked into patterns by similarity

C. UPSET:
Reminder of earlier A, B or C

B. SECONDARY:
Loss, emotional trauma

A. CORE:
Pain, unconsciousness, threat to survival

It is sometimes difficult to determine what similarities link these images from the past into patterned chains. In the regression work I have done I am always amazed at what the mind considers to be similar, and yet once the entire pattern is revealed, the similarity is obvious. If we hark back to the reptile, which is really the part of the brain primarily using this function, we see that the reptile will do its fight/flight/freeze set of behaviors at the slightest provocation when things are not normal. As stated earlier, it can afford to make many mistakes (false negatives) and still survive and therefore employs a rule of similarity something like, "Everything is the same as everything else, except not always" which makes it difficult to figure out.

So whenever the current environment is at all like anything in one of those strings of images where survival appeared to be threatened, the entire pattern is triggered. It comes up and is automatically replayed in its entirety in your current experience. When this occurs, you are technically upset, and in that upset everything you think, feel, say or do comes out of the stack of images. Your mood, your attitude about yourself and life, your emotions which are replays of old emotions, your body sensations, aches, pains, breathing rate, and what you do, all come out of the replayed images.

Now you may be throwing a tantrum in a more adult fashion, with adult reasons, and sophisticated verbal attacks, but it is a tantrum none the less and it is a mechanical replay of earlier incidents. Some time in your past you threw a tantrum and survived, so the reptilian part of the mind now says, "Similar situation, throw tantrum, you will survive." When you have gone through the replayed experience, this current incident gets added to the top of that stack as another tertiary incident, another similar upset in a long string. When you are in the middle of this upset, you are responding totally mechanically; **you are a machine acting out some earlier drama.**

By the time we reach adulthood, many things are going to remind us of aspects of past survival threatened incidents (A's, B's and C's). It is often the case that people are continually in one upset or another or several at once, and thus sleepwalking mechanically through life. This is the mechanism of all the dysfunctional behavior that ruins our lives and causes so much suffering. Before looking at what we can do about it, several more models are needed.

PERSONALITY FORMATION

How did I get to be the way I am? How did I form my personality, end up with the prejudices I have, or arrive at my world view? These questions take us to the thinking of the German philosopher Martin Heidegger, who wrote that "Each of us is born into an already existent conversation." This conversation includes what it means to be a human being existing in a particular time in history; why our family, religion, or race is better than the neighbors'; and an opinion about every imaginable thing. In order to survive, which means to fit in to our family and society, we take on this "already existent conversation," which becomes our world view.

Most of the time, we never even formulate a question because life around us is so "just the way it is" that we take it on, as they say in fishing—hook, line, and sinker. First we learn it in our family of origin: how to get attention (cry or be good), what constitutes love (tenderness or abuse). Does my voice count? What do I deserve?—the answers to every conceivable question a growing child might have in trying to figure out how to get along, be accepted and survive. The entire world view is just imbibed almost as if it had been picked up through the pores of our skin, by osmosis, and becomes the background to our lives, much like water must be to the fish.

Born into an already existing conversation

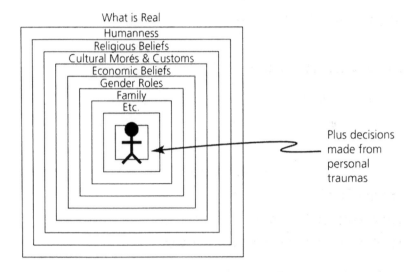

You would think that being a human being (as opposed to an animal) would be an innate part of our nature and not learned. However, there is a historic case of two infants in India in the late 1800's who were stolen by wolves at a very early age. When they were recaptured at around ten years old, one died and the other was never able to relearn how to be a functioning civilized human being. What this implies, besides the fact that almost all the content of your ego is learned, is that your personality is set in place at a very early age. Therefore it is not your fault as to how you ended up. Who you consider yourself to be is almost entirely a product of the environment into which you were born, along with some very basic genetic influences. You needed to take on and agree with almost all of the conversation into which you were born in order to fit in and survive. Finally, as we all know, it is very difficult to change this conditioning when we get older.

Another example of the powerful nature of this conversation into which we are born are the unexamined prejudices expressed through the language of young children, Arab against Jew, white against black, and so on. These ideas did not come from the children's experiences but from the stories handed down by their parents and the society into which they were born. Of course, the later acting-out of these same prejudices creates the kind of ugly chaos we see around the world and perpetuates the "truth" of these prejudices for both sides. And thus the conversation is passed to yet another generation.

This learned world view (within which is who you consider yourself to be) is really all part of one multi-dimensional, holographic, perceptual reality that your reptilian brain is constantly working to preserve. If the world view is harmful to actual life on the planet or to your relationships the reptilian brain will still cause the conditioned attitudes, ideas, and behaviors to survive in a kind of macabre ritual, like lemmings marching into the sea. In relationships you can witness people punishing their partners by withdrawing or verbally or physically abusing them in the hopes that their partner will give them love in the form that they crave. This is obviously a bad strategy for a loving relationship, but to the reptilian brain it is a proven, conditioned pattern of behavior, which seemed to be successful during childhood. On a planetary scale, it is easy to see the forces of power, control and greed that are consistent with a world view that "There isn't enough for everyone and I need to get more than enough to protect me and mine", ruining the very biosphere in which we all live and potentially hastening the demise of us all!

EXERCISE 5

The boxes I live within

(30 minutes to start, then open ended)

In your notebook write a list of your beliefs, prejudices, and notions about the way things are, especially those aspects of your world view which seem to justify you being the way you are. Admittedly, this is difficult to do because it is like a fish trying to see water when it is the element in which it swims. However, just starting to question the rightness of the way you see things will provide benefits. So spend some time at this and leave space in your notebook to add items as you see more of "the conversation into which you were born."

The best way to do this is to take whatever comes to mind, write it down, then analyze whether that belief or opinion is true for you. What is your view of men, of women, of aging, of money, of rich people, of material things, of other races, religions, and so on? Views that you "know" to be true, write them down. These are the beliefs of your world view, the map you have of the greater reality within which you operate. Each of us operates from our map most of the time, only infrequently dropping into a more expanded view of how it is. What is your map, your interpretation on the way things are?

My wife once accused me of being a male chauvinist, which I denied for a long time. After all, I was an *est* trainer; I treated everyone equally, I was too enlightened to operate out of that low level of prejudice. On and on I denied what she was trying to tell me about her experience of me, justifying my internal view of myself, and not wanting to be seen as wrong.

Finally, after much prompting on her part, I took an afternoon at the beach with my journal and wrote down every thought that came to me on the subject: I was glad I was a man, women were weaker, men were better, I was frightened of women, I felt not in control during sex, I hated feeling out of control, I blamed women for that, women were out of control with their emotions, etc., etc. Later that evening I returned home a much humbler husband with some sense of how my underlying, unexamined attitudes and beliefs had influenced my unexamined actions.

PERCEPTION

My thanks go to John Thompson of Human Factors for first introducing me to the following material.

In order to penetrate and really understand how we create the reality we find ourselves in, we need to understand the role of perception. I think it is fairly obvious that we can only deal with what we are aware of. This is the data in our lives (what

I notice within myself and what I am aware of outside myself) out of which we make selections and decisions, take actions, and thereby produce results. The question is, 'where does our awareness come from'? Or 'what shapes our awareness, such that we are aware of what we are aware of and not aware of other things'?

I grew up hearing the expression, "If I see it, I'll believe it." In fact I have subsequently found that our experienced reality is exactly the opposite. You will not even see what you don't already believe exists or have some possibility for its existence in your belief system. For example, you may not believe that UFOs exist, but your belief system has them as a possibility, so if one showed up on your lawn you would know what it was.

You know that a ghost is a holographic image that you could put your hand through, so while you might not believe in ghosts, you're prepared to see one. Outside of your beliefs and outside what you are aware of within those beliefs that constitute your entire reality, are the things that never even come onto your awareness screen. These things might be right in front of you, may even be affecting your physical, emotional or mental state, yet they are somehow filtered out. Somewhat like cancer-causing radiation: you don't know it is affecting you until you get the physical signs of cancer.

The current scientific explanation (somewhat simplified) is that the external world's sensory data (light, sound, particles, and so on) hits the body's sensory receptors, which in turn triggers nerve impulses that pass from the sensory receptor to the reptilian brain, activating or not activating the fear response we have already talked about. Part of activating the fear response is the activation of the limbic brain and its chemical/emotional systems. Signals then travel to the neo-cortex where each of us constructs, out of the many sensory inputs, a multi-sensory holographic 3D image we **experience as reality.**

By way of example, take seeing. The light from a light source bounces off an object and the altered wave/particle beam goes through the eye lens where it is inverted. It then hits the retina where it activates the rods and cones, which in turn initiate an electric signal through the optic nerve. These electric impulses jump a succession of synapse gaps on their way to the reptilian brain. Then after being precognitively filtered and checked for survival threat by the reptilian brain, the impulses are passed to the neo-cortex where an image is constructed that we experience as a visual form -"I am seeing X."

In the 1950's, in his attempt to understand the brain's functioning, Dr. Wilder Penfield conducted experiments using an electric probe to stimulate various parts of the neo-cortex. Patients, who did not need to be anesthetized because of the few tactile nerve cells in the brain itself, reported experiencing multi-sensory holographic virtual realities (memories) in great detail as if they were actually reliving them. So we know that this part of the brain actually constructs these images.

However if we now turn to what you can observe—and thereby know—directly through your experience, something slightly different from the above scientific explanation emerges.

EXERCISE 6

Experiencing my Perception

(15 minutes)

Close your eyes and listen to some sound outside your body. Where do you experience that sound? Where do you experience it in the total space of your reality? Is the sound in your head, between your ears somewhere, or would you say it is coming from somewhere experientially out there in space? I think that as you look you will experience it as being the latter. Forget the scientific explanation and what you learned about hearing; just observe what you know experientially.

Next, open your eyes and notice an object. Where do you have the visual experience of it being? Not behind your eyes, I suggest, but out in space where you say, "It is." As you notice more objects you might notice that in the realm of visual reality, the only difference between objects is difference in form and difference in location in the three dimensions of space.

The same is true for all five senses, although touching only occurs at the surface of the skin or within your body, and taste is in various places in your mouth, as smell is in the nostrils. Now it is important not to confuse the object itself that you are experiencing out there in space with the label or name you give it, or with your judgment or opinion about it, all of which are thoughts located around your body and not out there where you experience the object located.

What this tells us experientially (not logically or scientifically) is that this multi-sensory holographic reality, the only reality we know, the one we say, "I know this or that is true because I experience it" exists for us, in space, where we experience it being – all around us. As you examine this further, you might notice that your body is simply another visual form with tactile sensations, thoughts and emotions within it. It is a part of this larger multi-sensory holographic reality. It is not that "what you consider yourself to be" is separate from what you experience, but rather that what you consider yourself to be is within it. As you continue to observe what is so, rather than think about it, your direct experience should confirm this explanation. The entire scientific explanation may be based on the unexamined, mistaken assumption that "I am separate from everything out there" rather than I am a part of it all.

The next piece of information about this total experiential reality is that **each of us has our own version of reality** that is more or less different from others. Witness ten people filing accident reports about the same accident. You get ten variations, some as far afield as "she was black" versus "he was blond". Now these different multi-sensory holographic realities when looked at more closely seem to be **heavily biased toward a preferred version of reality.** This preferred version of reality is the "already existent conversation" we were born into as children, which we may have slightly modified in subsequent years and it is the filter making your "reality" different from others.

Here is an example. There is a classic experiment in which people agreed to wear glasses that inverted reality all the time. After at first seeing everything upside down, by the end of a week or more everyone reported that everything had returned to normal right side up! When they took the glasses off, things inverted once again, but this time it only took about half the time to re-correct to how they knew it was. The mind, with the help of the reptilian brain, is incredibly powerful in reinforcing this biased, preferred version of reality. It will ignore certain data, screening it out, or invent new data to fill in the blanks so as to create what we "know" is there.

Another example is the well-documented case of a "phantom limb". After amputation of a leg, the amputee often reports feeling sensations where the foot used to be, not at the stump where the nerve endings now end. Often, feeling these sensations, the patient forgets he no longer has a leg and tries to stand, only to discover his error.

A recent example of this sent to me by friends shows how the mind fills data in to get us to the preferred version of reality. *"Aoccdrnig to rscheearch at Cmabrigde Uinervtisy, it deosn't mttaer waht oredr the ltteers in a wrod are, the olny iprmoetnt thing is taht the frist and lsat ltteer be in the rghit pclae. The rset can be a ttoal mses and you can sitll raed it wouthit a porbelm. Tihs is bcuseae the mnid deos nto raed ervey lteter by istlef, but the wrod as a wlohe."* I might add that this is true for all the data coming into your sensors. There is some recent research that says we only need about ten percent raw data and the mind connects the dots, so to speak, just like a computer decompression program, to create our total multi-sensory reality.

Vase/Two Faces

In viewing optical illusions like the vase/two faces, it is not so much that we have the power to switch our perception from one "what I see" to another, but that our mind is doing that kind of selective seeing all the time. Further, if we are attached to a certain way we know the world is, the reptilian brain will make sure that we only receive evidence supporting that particular view.

EXERCISE 7

First Belief, then Experience

Read the words in the pyramid out loud.

Now, read it again.

Did you notice the second "the", or did you just read it as "a bird in the hand, xxxx"? We tend to not see evidence that is right in front of us, evidence that is definitely coming in through our sensory preceptors but gets screened out before the reality formation process takes place in the neo-cortex, because "we already know how it is" – only faces or only vases. When you really start to understand this phenomena, it makes you question whether anything you know is really the way you say it is, or just something you have learned along the way and have been selectively reinforcing ever since. It should put a big question mark on your righteousness!

CHAPTER THREE

Who I Consider Myself to Be

INTERIM SUMMARY

So what we have is you, your Self, a Being, partially lost in its ego identity, replaying patterns of conditioned behaviors whenever the mechanical and not very discriminatory part of your brain feels in any way threatened. As you grow up, what you consider yourself to be may change, but the mechanism that ensures the survival of your ego, the reptilian brain, continues on defending who you consider yourself to be (your personality, your body, your athletic prowess, your money, your ideas).

This defense comes in the form of making yourself right and others wrong (arguments), justifying your mental position and/ or your behavior, dominating others or avoiding domination by others. These are all variations on the theme of "I feel better than or less than others" which is entirely the ego's game.

There are two important aspects of this behavior. The first is that the reptilian brain does not distinguish between your body and your opinions, beliefs, and worldview. It will equally defend whatever you are attached to, which is to say whatever you consider yourself to be. The second aspect is the manner in which the reptilian brain screens out evidence that does not fit your worldview. It can also add evidence that does fit, so that you continually see what you already believe and know to be true and right.

Therefore we find ourselves living in a self-fulfilling prophecy, a repeat of some earlier, learned reality, that as children we had little choice over. In fact in order to survive, which to an infant means being held, fed, and paid attention to, and in order to fit in to an ever-widening social group, to not be rejected, meant taking on the whole conversation we were born into. This includes of course the dynamic of rebelling against certain aspects, or rejecting certain aspects of the reality through your behavior.

The process of rejecting, or rebelling against, or resisting is just another way of confirming and reinforcing the reality of the very thing you are resisting. This is why it is said, "You get what you resist. Or resistance causes persistence." Thus your entire reality, your "worldview" as I am calling it, which has within it your personality, is maintained and defended in order for your ego to survive.

Have you ever tried to give another person a suggestion as to how they might solve their problem or get out of an unhappy circumstance? Often you find that the suggestion doesn't seem to get through to them no matter how much effort you put into the argument. While we haven't discussed all that is necessary to fully understand this dynamic, your suggestion somehow threatens their view of themselves and the reality in which they live. Their reptilian brain just won't let your "good idea" in. Even if their unhappiness and suffering continues, their reptilian brain continues doing its job of causing who they consider themselves to be to survive. Please note, happiness has nothing to do with survival as far as the ego is concerned. In fact it seems to be the first thing given up. Why this occurs is covered next.

THE CORE CONSIDERATION

The following information I have known about since Thomas A. Harris's book, *I'm OK, You're OK* came out in the 1970's. However, I was not holding the information in a way that gave me any real ability or power to transform my experience. It was not until recently that I saw that I had been holding the information as content in an old victim paradigm rather than as the context for the reality within which I was living. Then many of my confusions about why I did what I did and continuously created the cycles of unhappiness in my life finally became clear. I hope by my sharing this key understanding with you, you will not have to go through the many years of suffering and unhappiness that I went through as I struggled to figure out how I was creating my life.

Many of the original insights came through some very painful work I did on myself in the 1980's and 90's. I here wish to acknowledge Bob Hoffman and his 10-day Quadrinity Process in which I participated at two different times when my wife and I were struggling through separations. Thanks also to Lazaris for the intense 4-day Original Pain and Shame workshop I did with Concept Synergy. And finally for the wonderful support I received from the Total Integration Institute through the work they do called Domain Shift and Living Freedom. However, the confirmation for this next model of "who you consider yourself to be" came through many sessions guiding people back to early childhood and birth experiences. These regression experiences with others assured me it wasn't just some odd way I was wired.

Remember, the mind, as we have defined it, is a complete multi-sensory holographic record of everything that we have experienced since birth (and perhaps earlier). These early images are difficult for us to remember because they include the unconsciousness associated with the physical and emotional traumas, and as you get closer and closer to them there is a tendency to go to sleep. I have experienced intrauterine images as well as images from apparently prior lifetimes as have many people with whom I have worked, but it is not necessary to accept this premise in order to follow the argument and get value from this model.

Whether these images are imagined or actual records is somewhat irrelevant as their experiential existence and one's ability to observe them is the only thing that in any real sense matters. As I will explain later, when images from the past are observed, rather than relived as an automatic replay, the power they hold over you in the reality you are creating disappears. So do the automatic patterns of dysfunctional behaviors derived from those images.

Imagine with me the following: it is not far off from what almost all of us went through. At some point in your development as a fetus in your mother's womb, there was a generalized experience of existing. You were part of your mother, her heart beating in the background, her moods transferred to you chemically through the blood, which carried both oxygen and food. It was a time in which everything was taken care of; you were fully nurtured in a floating environment of muted lights, soft sounds and comfort, "full womb service" so to speak! This experience of connection, of being fully nurtured, accepted, and loved becomes a significant reference experience—one we keep trying to repeat in the future.

As the moment of birth gets nearer, the quarters became tighter and more constricting. Finally, through some rather violent contractions, you are forced down a tunnel, which is inherently too small for you. Your bones would be crushed were they not so soft and malleable. You have no control over this process. No matter what you do the sensation of constriction and the feeling of helplessness is overpowering, as are the accompanying emotions of panic and rage.

Birth is definitely one of those physical traumas, which includes plenty of unconsciousness and apparent threat to survival. Suddenly you are in the world of bright lights, sharp harsh sounds, lower temperature, and abrasive materials on your skin. If you didn't get assisted out with forceps around your forehead and temples, you at least got a welcoming whack to the small of your back. You are here in this world, alone for the first time (at least in this lifetime), separate from the experience of connection so recently left behind.

If you were an unwanted baby, there might have been physical abortion attempts (more trauma) and confusing messages from your mother in terms of emotions and moods (emotional trauma). All of these experiences would have been stored as multi-sensory holographic images by the mind and included in the category of "necessary to survival." These will be repeated in some form later in life because after all, by going through what you went through, thinking what you thought, and doing what you did, you did survive!

No matter how gentle your birth—into water, with dimmed lights and muted sounds—at some point each of us reaches the stage where for some period of time we are not getting our needs met. We may be hungry, have gas pains, be colicky, feverish, wet, cold, alone, crying, yelling, throwing a tantrum, feeling we are going to die, yet no one comes to take care of us. To a small baby this is not a minor issue. In those moments it is an entire bodily-felt experience consuming all our limited awareness. This incident and others like it are definitely considered threats to survival by the reptilian brain.

At this stage of our development, we are what developmental psychologists call existing in a totally self- or ego-centered reality. In other words, the distinction between my self and others is just emerging. There is little or no awareness of what might be going on with another person; all experience relates to what this means about me. In that extended moment when our needs are not being met and we are no longer experiencing being nurtured by our mother or care giver, we make a critical life altering decision.

At that point we decide something which, until we unravel it later in life, is going to affect every aspect of our future. At that moment in a primitive, non-verbal way, we decide that the reason "she" is not here taking care of me has nothing to do with her agenda, and everything to do with me. We decide, "I am Not OK." This "Not OKness" has many variations as we get older and are able to further define our Not OKness. Some of these are: I am bad; I am flawed; I am not enough; I am undeserving; I am unlovable; there is something missing in me. For if I were OK, she certainly would be here to take care of me and I wouldn't be experiencing all these terrible body sensations, feelings and thoughts.

The core incidents out of which this pivotal declaration is made wouldn't necessarily have to have been birth and the experiences of abandonment that followed shortly after birth. It is just that most people have this in common. No matter how attentive your mother was, at some time she wasn't there. You were not conscious enough to really know what was going on, so you determined in your own mind from the data available and your egocentric point of view what was so.

Other types of incidents which equally serve are childhood accidents and sicknesses where you ended up in a strange, alien hospital. Or there may have been abuse, deprivation, or any other incident containing pain, unconsciousness and threat to survival. Usually incidents of this type that occur later tend to reinforce and perhaps further define the decision of Not OKness already declared.

This fundamental decision, which is in the form of a declaration "I am ....." becomes the core experience of who we consider ourselves to be. As we will see, in a very bizarre way we defend and maintain this identity while at the same time trying to prove to the world that what we consider as a fundamental fact is not true about us. As we will see, this Not OKness becomes not only the driving force behind our outward personality, but also the fundamental truth about the reality in which we live.

The useful model here is: the Observer Self, our divine aspect, after feeling at oneness with mother, has the experience of being separate and not nurtured along with all the accompanying body sensations and emotions of rage, panic, and terror. In that extended moment, your Self makes a declaration, "I am Not OK," and then later puts together a personality on top of that declaration to prove that that isn't true. The personality, the outer act (as in a role in a play) continually tries to prove to the rest of the world that "I am OK" in order to get the nurturing you feel you need from others. We keep looking for the experience of being connected, taken care of, filled up, nurtured, and unconditionally loved that is so reminiscent of the womb.

It is in this development of the outer act that we develop our strategies for success. Often these strategies are derived from roles already played by our parents so it is not as if you have to invent too much that is new. These character traits even go so far as to include patterns of abuse. "I am acting just like you did with me. Now will you finally give me the love I crave since I'm so much like you?" cries the wounded child in an adult body to a now dead parent. Bob Hoffman called this negative love syndrome and it explains how the sins of the parents are passed down to the children, generation after generation.

Therefore I will be good to get your love, mommie and daddy. I will do the right things, accept what you say, try to meet your expectations in my accomplishment, be the best, help around the house, be just like you, anything, to try and get unconditionally loved and accepted. If I can't get love I will at least take some symbols of love, like attention, and if I can't get attention with positive actions, then negative actions will have to do. Because any attention is better than no attention, which feels like abandonment and rejection and harkens back to that terrible time when I first decided I wasn't OK.

This outside persona that is presented to the world has an inner experience of being something of a charade, at its core false, because who I really am is Not OK. And it is for this reason that no amount of acknowledgement later in life, no amount of accomplishment, no amount of money or possessions, no amount of people telling you they love you, or admire and respect you, gives you the lasting experience you are looking for. This outward personality has often been referred to as **who I am pretending to be,** which in turn covers over **who I am afraid I am** (which by the way at the deepest level I **know** I am) and all of this makes up who I consider myself to be. This is the structure of the ego.

The ego

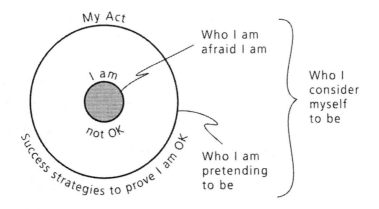

We will come back to this model after a discussion on how we create the reality in which we live and again later in a lengthy discussion on intimate relationships.

Chapter Four

Reality Creation

In order to understand how our declarations such as "I am Not OK" as well as other subsequent decisions about ourselves, other people, and life in general actually manifest, we need to examine the nature of reality itself.

I was first introduced to the following material in the summer of 1972 by Werner Erhard when I participated in the *est* training in Aspen, Colorado. I had just returned from India and was wearing white pajamas, a sandalwood japamala around my neck, long hair, and a holier-than-thou attitude. I was gracing my fellow participants with my presence in the seminar as I was on the path to becoming America's first saint! The only reason, I told myself, that I was attending this training was to understand my little brother and his wife who were stringing together words like "space" and "responsible" in ways I had never heard before.

I remember sitting in the back row of seats with my friend John Denver, making comments about this slick encyclopedia salesman named Werner. Little did I realize what a profound impact this training would have on me, or how I would change my life as a result. At the end of the two weekends I was convinced that the *est* training was the fast track to enlightenment. Here was a technology that could eliminate the unwanted patterns and programming and allow me to create more love, health, happiness and full self-expression.

While I then went to Tecate, Mexico to study yoga with Indra Devi and subsequently ran the Sai Baba center in Los Angeles for a few months, when Werner put out the call for people to become trainers that fall of 1972, I signed up and subsequently joined the *est* staff in January 1973. During the next seven years I trained more than 50,000 people and experienced the enormous satisfaction of watching people transform before my eyes, knowing that I had contributed to that transformation.

In the chapter on perception we learned that each of us experiences slightly different versions of reality. This ever-changing experience, at any moment in time, includes both what we might call, "your internal experience" and "your external experience." Your internal experience includes body sensations, emotions, thoughts, ideas, images of the past, fantasies of the future, judgments, opinions, and of course labels and names for things. Your external experience includes the entire multi-sensory universe from the smallest organism you can detect to the most distant stars you can see, and within that spectrum includes the visual form of your body.

This is all you really truly know in this moment. It is your truth in this moment of Now. If you say, "But my experience keeps changing," then you are comparing this moment of **actual** experience to a memory/record of a prior moment and only know that a change occurred through the comparison. The point is that each of us has our own private experience that is real to us even if we sometimes question its validity (the question just becoming another thought in our internal experience) and whether or not others agree or disagree with it. "This is the way it is for me in this moment, this is my real experience, and it includes my entire universe as I experience it in this moment (along with the people who are agreeing or disagreeing!)".

Sometimes, however, you find that what you thought was real turned out to be a mistaken perception. In the past people thought the world was flat, now few do, or that the sun went around the earth, or that you bled people for health. Perhaps you can recall an example from your own life, where you realized you had a mistaken perception. In that instance, what is it that changed your mind? What is the proof that convinced you that what you thought you experienced is no longer true and that some other experience is now the way it is?

If I showed you physically, would you accept whatever it was as real? Most people would say that the ultimate proof for what is real is that it is physical. At times it is as if you had been deceived by the magician's slight of hand trick. However, once you see how it works physically, you are no longer fooled by the illusion you previously thought was real.

By definition, for something to be physical means you can sense its existence through your five senses, or some combination of your physical senses. Or you can measure it using a physical device, like a microscope or telescope, which extends your rather limited senses. If you can't measure whatever it is, it is usually dismissed as not being real. Does that mean then that the essence of physicality is also physical?

Scientists have been looking for the stuff out of which all reality is made for as long as there have been scientists. They have continued to push the limits by exploring ever-smaller particles through the use of ever larger and more powerful measuring devices like mile-long particle accelerators. While the hope remains of finding reality's fundamental element, it is very disconcerting because the more the scientists look, the less they find. And what they do find is indefinite and expressed as a probability function surrounded by an enormous amount of nothing. This would say that the substance of physical reality is very non-physical, at least extremely non-solid.

Yet to prove something is real we still test it for physicalness: meaning we are able to measure it. By definition, all physical objects have dimensions, length, width, depth, some mass, and exist somewhere in space even if for only a short period of time. So we could say that something is real if it is measurable. Examining measurability leads us into the world of agreed-upon standards and the comparisons of one thing to another.

The physical object we are trying to prove exists is measured by comparing it to some other physical object experts agree is the standard weight, distance, temperature, or time. What makes something the standard is that someone in authority, or a group (like PhD scientists from Berkeley) that people agree has authority declares it as "the standard." Perhaps it is the king who says, "The length of my foot will now be the standard foot and three feet, the length of my stride will be a yard."

So somewhere there is or was a physical standard that this new physical object is being compared to. Therefore, that which proves something is physical and really real is something else which is itself physical. It is like two blocks of wood bumping up against one another, each proving the other exists! Which one is really real? All that can be said is that they each in turn agree with the existence of the other, but that is not a definitive test for the existence of physical reality itself!

The resolution to this quandary of what is the essence of reality is that reality is not made up of some fundamental physical thing but of agreement itself. What we call "reality" is a function of agreement. This means the more agreement something has the more real it is. And something is ultimately real when the entire physical universe agrees with its existence in that nothing else physical can occupy that particular place in space at that moment in time.

Looking at what we call reality from a metaphysical perspective leads to a conversation about the dual nature of the world in which we live. This is the argument which says everything is relative and that nothing exists without its opposite. You can't have up without down, inside without outside, big without small, or black without white.

Imagine being in a world of only white. Pretty soon you would lose all sense of yourself since of course you are also white and there is nothing that is not white. In this world of all white there wouldn't even be white as we know it, since there would be no relative reference point with which to distinguish white from something else. In order for something to exist, there must be something else it is not. This something else in its simplest form is the null set—the "not X" which agrees with the existence of "X."

The "not white" which agrees with the existence of white, the "not ball" which includes everything that is not the ball and confirms the very existence of the ball itself. This fundamental level of agreement is the substance of the reality in which we live. In this dualistic reality, the more agreement something has, the more real it is, with the ultimate reality being physical, since everything else which is physical now agrees with its physical existence.

Combining the above arguments into a useful model we conclude: At an experiential level we have our own experience, which is multi-sensory, all-inclusive and unique to each of us. This multi-sensory universe, while totally real to each of us, is nonetheless made up of gradations in what we call "reality." The determining factor for these gradations is the amount of agreement each aspect in this multi-sensory universe has.

In terms of manifestation, or the process of making something "real," new ideas arise out of nothing/everything and progressively gain agreement. The amount of agreement gained determines its degree of "reality" in our world with the ultimate agreement level being physicalness.

Here is a general example. The mere hint of an idea emerges out of the nothing/everything soup. As it gets clearer in your mind, other thoughts agree with it. In other words, it starts to fit into the already existent conversation and set of beliefs in your own mind—thus adding agreement to the thought. Now as you speak about the thought to others, the thought is moving into the agreement reality of other people. Have you ever noticed that as you spoke an idea to others it actually started to get clearer, more defined, or more precise? As more and more people agree with the idea (disagreement works just as well in terms of speaking to the existence of something since you can't disagree with what doesn't exist) it becomes more and more "real."

When a whole community agrees, the idea becomes a general practice, custom, or belief. These ideas that a whole community agrees upon are no longer flimsy ideas, but can exist as very powerful realities influencing both life and death. Justified by the reality of their beliefs, Christians have gone on crusades to kill infidels in the name of brotherly love, and men have killed female family members for shaming their family name, all with the approval of the community at large. In these ways the custom or belief moves into physicalness through the actions of its adherents.

A more specific example is the creation of a building. An architect starts with an idea for a building. It may be fully formed in his mind, but it is not yet a reality as far as the world is concerned. Talking about the new building and making drawings all add agreement to the idea. If he is able to convince a client to put up the money (which is simply paper or ones and zeros in a bank's computers that everyone agrees have value and can therefore be traded for goods and services) then his idea has taken another step down the path of adding agreement to it and hence making it more real. As the money buys detailed drawings, laborer's time (actions) and construction materials, more agreement is added to the idea, until finally the building stands as a reality.

Here is an example of the many different levels of agreement-based reality. In a court room in the specially designed building with impressive columns called the court house, with one person designated as the judge (by agreement within a complex interwoven societal structure of law schools, laws, policemen, and legislators), the lawyers for the plaintiff and defense (having gone to law school to learn the agreements by which the game is played and gaining agreement from the law community that they know these agreements by passing the bar exam), abiding by rules of law (agreements established by supreme court judges and politicians) and referring to precedents selectively chosen from past cases (here the past gives continuity and agreement to the present decisions), argue the case before twelve jurors off the street who by agreement are not trained in much of anything!

If these twelve jurors agree you are guilty in that court room (not at a bar down the street) then you are "really" guilty and will "really" hang. It is irrelevant that you experience you didn't do it. Or if they say you didn't do it, you walk free, again regardless of what you experienced really happened (there are people who call up the police station after every major crime saying they did it). The tendency is to think that there really was something that happened, rather than everyone with their own unique experiences, agreeing and disagreeing with each other, or by some set of agreements one person having the power to say, "My experience is the right one."

Everything we call "real" is part of what the eastern metaphysical tradition calls the Illusion, because it is a function of agreement to a greater or lesser degree, constantly changing, and impermanent. Most people find the tenuous nature of this Grand Illusion really upsetting. They would rather have the false security of believing that there is some ultimate, big deal truth behind all of this apparent reality and that their beliefs, their interpretations, and certainly what they experience are part of that truth.

There was a time in which almost everyone agreed the world was flat and operated accordingly; now further physical evidence has altered that belief. But how do you know you are not just as deluded by your notions of what is real as were the majority of people in Columbus's time? To not hold a degree of skepticism about even your most dearly loved ideas and beliefs is to live in an arrogant fantasy. At the same time, to get anything accomplished we must be committed to some aspect of that experience (the architect's idea for the building) and masterfully manage the illusion, this huge agreement field all around us.

Manifestation naturally flows from BE to DO to HAVE. Applying this BE -> DO -> HAVE model to how each of us creates reality we see that thought is initiated into the reality-making stream in its most pure form through declaration: "I am ...". But any thought to which you are committed, a creative idea, a decision, a belief, or even an insight or scientific discovery can initiate the process. This is the critical BE part, from which all else flows.

A Being, in its god-like capacity, declaring how things are, out of which comes actions, and from those DOs come the results and the things we HAVE in life. We already know how to do this as each of us long ago declared, "I am Not OK" and created an entire life reality from that declaration. That one was done unconsciously. Now it is time to create what you want consciously.

One of the blocks to creating what you want is that you can't create a new reality in the space of one that you have already created. This is the reason most affirmations don't work. It is like trying to build the architect's building when an old building already exists on the chosen site. First you have to tear down the old building to make room for the new. In the reality-creating business that we are all in, the ability to observe is your tool for removing the old. And declaration is what creates the new.

I ran into the concept of sponsoring thoughts (as in underlying beliefs) for every level of reality in the books Conversations with God by Neale Donald Walsch. It was when I realized that all declarations become sponsoring thoughts that much of the material in this book that had been with me for years started to come together as a complete and powerful model.

In the process of clearing patterns (getting rid of the old buildings), when you come in contact with and observe the original declaration/decision you made as a baby or child the whole pattern that is held together by and based on that sponsoring thought will disappear. This includes the emotions, their subsequent actions and the results they create that are all a function of the sponsoring thought underneath that pattern in your reality. This means that the pattern exists simultaneously at all lesser gradation levels of the agreement reality. Therefore, if you can deal with the pattern at the more subtle levels, you don't have to struggle to dismantle the more physical manifestations. This is why insights into your conditioned way of being are so powerfully liberating. And why new realities are as available as your ability to declare them into existence.

By way of example: I decided as a little child that I was not good enough to get the love and nurturing I wanted and needed—there was something (I wasn't sure what) missing in me. At the same time, I decided (by agreeing with the prevailing conversation of the times) that I lived in a world in which there wasn't enough for everyone. In me, this produced a personality that has excelled at achievements and continually tried to prove "I was the best."

No matter how much I achieved however, it was never quite enough to truly feel satisfied, fulfilled and totally OK about myself. The context of this reality, its sponsoring thought, and therefore my core belief about myself, was "I am not enough." This produced a constant, gnawing, underlying sense of dissatisfaction, which I have been plagued with my whole life. I have done everything to overcome this.

I was competitive with my brothers and later with every other male to get what I perceived as the limited love and nurturing that was available. This cost me love and affinity with them. I was a compulsive controller in any situation in which I felt remotely competent under the assumption that by being in control I would emerge the shining winner. I would go to sleep in meetings I couldn't control. I had to do life all on my own, was surrounded by incompetent people, and angry about it. Also, I was easily upset, getting hurt and angry, when someone would try to give me feedback, especially a woman. I would go into a funk, feeling down about myself and depressed and push her away, thus losing the connection and love that I so much wanted.

Later I realized that all the emotions, the emptiness, hurt, anger and depression, while feeling very real at the time, were in fact a product of the reality I had created through my own early declaration, "I am not enough, living in a world of not enough." Such a shock when I realized I was the one making me feel badly. Situations and other people can trigger the feelings but all reactive feelings come from the way you are holding yourself, or have positioned yourself, in your reality. Once I finally observed this dynamic and the decisions I had made, I was able to let go of the pattern.

Suddenly my need to control, my dysfunctional competitiveness, my compulsion to achieve, and my inability to receive feedback disappeared as well. Then and only then, was I able to declare a new, more beneficial reality for myself. I now live in a world where there is enough for everyone (even though some evidence may appear contrary) and I am sufficient and OK the way I am. This has allowed me to create the experience of being happy and satisfied.

This does not mean that I never have the same feelings and inclinations to achieve or control; it is just that by knowing my personality patterns and being on the lookout for situations in which they might arise, I am free from having to act on them. And the longer I am free and the more I exercise my choice to not behave in the old ways, the less hold the pattern has over me and the less it actually even arises.

Sometimes when you see a pattern clearly and are able to let it go, there is some residual "agreement reality" still remaining—like friends who still want you to be the old way. Given whatever pattern they are acting out, they have a vested interest in your remaining the way you were so they can continue being the way they were. You have been in a dance together. But when you change, they have to change because of the very nature of the agreement reality you are co-creating together. Usually, once you have stopped feeding the old pattern with your life energy (attitudes, thoughts, words and actions), the agreement field shifts rapidly and the old problems are easily dissolved.

SECOND EDITION COMMENTS

As part of creating reality in our time/space bound world, it is necessary to take a stand for what you want. This means taking a position, defining yourself and your beliefs, saying, "I am this or that". Now it is very easy when you do this to slip into the old "right/wrong" game in which by taking a position you hold it in such a way that makes other positions wrong, or that in the way you communicate about your position you make others wrong and yourself (now your ego position) right.

The key is to recognize that we all tend to do this through the survival mechanisms previously described in Chapter Two and therefore to learn to hold our positions differently. This is tricky as it involves holding your position, taking your stand, without too much attachment, or what I would call "holding your position loosely, or softly."

If you are going to make a difference in the world, to change something through taking a stand, then two additional elements must be present: commitment and persistence. By being committed you are in some regards by definition attached and the more passionate you are about the subject, the easier it is for your ego to identify with the position (this stand of yours in the world) and feel it must be defended. This is not to say "live a life devoid of passion" because you need some of that emotional energy, that passion, to attract to you what you want and after all, where is the fun if you can't have something you are passionate about?

In addition, you have to hold your position for a certain length of time to allow our agreement based reality time to form around your position and make it "real." The more the commitment, the more the passion, and the longer the time simply means you must be more vigilant and aware of the ego's tendency to slip into the right/wrong game. This can happen either overtly through spoken judgments and criticisms or just internally in your own mind. Either way you end in an alienated world surrounded by more and more of the "enemy" having given up the love, harmony and connection with others that would otherwise be possible.

What do I mean by "holding your position loosely, or softly". It is something I first came across in the martial art of Aikido in which one drops into one's center and in a very relaxed way holds a position on the mat and deals with all incoming attacks by turning the energy of the attacker back against himself. Translating this to the metaphysical world of manifestation involves three elements: clear intention, being in the flow, and being in the moment. I will address each element.

Clear intention

More than anything else, I have found it is important to know what I want. The clearer I am, the faster things manifest for me now. Once clear on my intention, and to a certain extent generating some desire, or excitement for having it, then I need to "let it go" or kind of "let it be" in an unattached way so as to let the universe do it's part and to allow me to experience the miracle of getting what I want in perhaps a way I could never have foreseen. For this magic to happen I need to be open, soft, receptive, and allowing. I attempt to not rivet my focus on this image I have as being the only way in which my desires will be fulfilled and thus being tight and rigid in my stance, but rather always having my intention in the background, an image of what I desire, held loosely, trusting that the universe will deliver what I need next to make my intention manifest.

For much of my life, I have been unable to figure out what I want, living in a kind of dissatisfied confusion, while trying to fit into other people's expectations so as to gain the love or approval I felt I needed. Since what I said I wanted didn't really come from my authentic desires, I often did not get what I intended and I was so rigid that I failed to let in what I did get. I had been disappointed so many times I just wasn't willing to go through the disappointment one more time. "Why bother?" To be able to rehabilitate my ability to actually put forth my desires, I needed to give up trying so hard to please others when it meant sublimating my own needs and desires.

Being in the flow

Without being open and receptive, it is impossible to be in the flow of the universal life force that we live in and co-create with. It is in the nature of the law of attraction that the more open and receptive we are, while still maintaining our clarity and focus on what we desire, the more ways we will experience interactions, ideas, and situations contributing to the manifestation of our desires.

One of the ways this works for me is by constantly adjusting the order in which I do various aspects of "things I want to get done " according to what happens and who or what shows up throughout the day, week, or year. The more flexible I am, the less attached to how things occur, or even the part I need to play in their occurrence or to whom goes the credit, the more magical and easier my life seems. If something doesn't go according to my original plan, I practice not getting upset, trusting it is for my benefit somehow, and adjusting my time sequence or perhaps even my priorities. All of this requires the third element.

Being in the moment

As I have said through out this book, the only time you can change anything is in this moment of Now. The only element over which you have total control is you and the only way to change you and your reality is to show up differently, to BE different. So in the end getting what you want is a combination of Being all the aspects you desire, clear in your intention, and also taking a stand to be open, soft, receptive, a good listener, appreciative, loving, etc. I find that "being in the moment" means how I show up with every person with whom I interact. To help me get "here" I often notice my breath and feel my feet on the floor and only then begin the interaction. Not only does this become immensely satisfying, but opens the possibility for the magic of co-creation—the ultimate win/win.

CHAPTER FIVE

The Fundamental Choice

The fundamental choice for each of us is whether we are going to reside within this multi-sensory holographic universe we experience as a victim (at the effect of it) or as somehow responsible for causing it. What is the difference and which stance do we take? This interactive dialogue came out of my days as a trainer with Lifespring (a human potential movement training similar to est) and later in the work I did with business executives as part of the Human Factors team (an off shoot of Lifespring with focus on team building and corporate culture change).

The beginning of this discussion takes us to the definition of ATTITUDE, which I define as a mental position about something. The objects you have an attitude about vary and perhaps your attitudes vary as well. It is also true that you can change an attitude even though it may be difficult at any given time. For example, you may have had one attitude as a teenager about making out in cars and quite another now as an adult with teenage children. Similar event, different attitude! I am sure you have had days where you got up on the wrong side of the bed and this attitude about life affected almost everything that you experienced in a negative way until your attitude changed.

Often the change comes about as a result of some occurrence, like your lover called. Nevertheless, the attitude did change and thereafter life appeared and was experienced differently. Attitudes affect your moods, the possibilities you experience mentally, your creativity, your energy, and consequently the actions you take and the results those actions produce—so attitudes are very powerful reality creators. The analogy would be the rose colored glasses that once put on make the whole world look rosy.

With regard to individual reality as it is experienced, there are two mutually exclusive attitudes we must choose between at the most etheric level of our existence: being "at the effect of" or being "at cause for" our reality. Now I am not necessarily advocating the truth of any one choice, as if there is a right one and a wrong one, only that there are these two mental positions and that there are significant consequences to each side of the choice.

The definition of being AT EFFECT: *I hold the mental position that I am disconnected and separate from this circumstance or situation in my reality. Things just happen to me. I hold the belief that there is nothing I can do to change this circumstance or situation.* An analogy would be that you are a rock in a stream bed that has a controlled dam upstream. When "they" open the dam and let more water out, you, the rock, get picked up and rolled downstream. As the water subsides, you land where you land and you either like or dislike it according to the circumstances you now find yourself in and your preferences for those circumstances. But you have nothing to do with where you land and no power to change the circumstances or, I might add, your reaction to them.

The definition of being AT CAUSE: *I hold the mental position that I am connected to this circumstance or situation as I now experience it. I hold the belief and therefore am open to discovering how my actions or non-actions as well as my perceptual conditioning have contributed to this circumstance or situation being the way it is for me. Furthermore, I believe I have some degree of power to change this situation if I so choose.*

If you look into your life I believe you will find situations in which you would say "I was *at effect* there" and others in which you could say, "In that situation, I was *at cause.*"

EXERCISE 8

At Cause/At Effect

(40 minutes)

In your notebook take two pages and label one page *At Effect* and the other *At Cause* and then draw a line down the middle of each page. Now on the left side of the appropriate page list the various incidents and aspects of your life that are in each category. If you are not sure, dissect the incident or aspect until you can say, "For this part I was *at effect* and for these parts I was *at cause.*" Include incidents from the past, your current relationships, your experience of poverty or abundance, your job, your free time, and your reactions to the things that occur in your life. Please make those lists before going on to the second part of this exercise.

Step two: On the right side of each page, write the emotions, feelings and thoughts you experienced arising in conjunction with that particular attitude.

Your lists might look something like this:

At Effect

Incidents and aspects of my life	Emotional Content
• my husband/wife's moods	sad
• how the boss treats me	helpless
• how our department is treated by others in the company	angry
	depressed
• my husband/wife's spending habits	irritated
• our continual lack of money	hateful
• my daughter/son's attitude about school	vengeful
• an incident where someone robbed me	low energy
	confused
	discouraged
	afraid
	constricted

At Cause

Incidents and aspects of my life	Emotional content
• what we do when I go fishing with my buddies	happy
	powerful
• what I contribute to the family	satisfied
• how well I play the guitar	joyful
• my accomplishments at work and the contributions they have made	at peace
	worthwhile
• whether I deal with my daughter/son's attitude or not	guilty*
	self-expressive
• the times when I have obviously made my wife/husband happy	creative
• my physical condition	energized
• how I spend my "extra" money	convinced I can accomplish more
• losing money on an investment	expansive

*As when things don't work out. Guilt will be examined as a special case on page 123, in Part Four of Chapter Six.

When you look at human motivation, I think it is obvious that people always take actions that they think at that moment will promise less pain and/or more satisfaction. I got married because it looked like I would be happier with this person than without her. I got divorced for the same reason! This applies even to seemingly minor behaviors like changing your position in a chair—away from discomfort toward more comfort. In summarizing the two lists above, we could say that the emotional experience associated with being *at cause* has the possibility of producing satisfaction although there is no guarantee. On the other hand, being *at effect* (along with its righteous complaining) produces dissatisfaction or at best some momentary relief from the underlying fear.

In life there are payoffs and costs to every action and this includes taking a particular attitude. If it were clear to you that you had a choice of attitude and that along with the attitude comes certain emotional experiences, why would you ever choose to be *at effect*? The cost of being *at effect* is the dissatisfaction and unhappiness it produces. But what is the payoff? What could you possibly be getting out of it? On the other hand, the payoff for being *at cause* is potentially the experience of satisfaction and full self-expression that all of us say we want. But what is its cost?

To answer these questions we must return to our ego's core fear which is to re-experience the abandonment with all the accompanying intense emotions and body sensations. These are the experiences out of which the decision/declaration "I am Not OK" was made. And it is this Not OKness which becomes the source of all subsequent feelings of shame. For the ego, this is the one thing it can't allow you to fully experience or you might cease to exist and die. Also, the avoidance of this negative experience and childhood conclusion has been the driving force behind the façade that now represents your outward personality. Therefore the ego will try to keep it all intact in performing its survival job. The situation that might lead to this experience of abandonment and consequent annihilation would be to be blamed for screwing things up. The humiliation, shame, and rejection that would follow are perceived by the ego as major threats to survival.

Therefore the payoff for taking an *at effect* or victim stance in the world is that you are able to play it safe (by not standing out, by fitting in) and therefore not be blamed, "Hey, it wasn't my fault." Thus the ego's looking-good image and its "I'm Not OK" decision survive. It is obvious by observing your own and other's behavior that the ego is much more interested in survival than in happiness since the opportunities for happiness and satisfaction that come with being *at cause* seem to be the first thing given up. This runs counter to what we say we want: "But, I **really** want to be happy".

On the other hand, taking the stance "I am responsible for what is occurring in my life," for being *at cause*, the payoff is the possibility of really being happy. However, the cost is the risk that you will be blamed and therefore have to experience your core fears while refraining from defending or justifying yourself, i.e. refraining from returning to an *at effect* posture. As you observe these feelings associated with ridicule and rejection, you will witness the release of your ego's power over you and the dysfunctional aspects of your ego will disappear. This sounds like just what you, your Self, would most like to do, but it is scary and will reactivate your ego's nastiest defense patterns.

Unless you take a conscious stance of being *at cause*, the default position will always be, being *at effect*. The reason for this is that the conversation we are born into is almost entirely one based on being a victim. We are victims of a father god who we must supplicate in order to get his approval. We are *at the effect* of our parents, teachers, and those who seem to hold all the knowledge while we are growing up. At best we can be good little boys and girls who do whatever we are told to do.

In addition, society has made the implicit promise that if you gain certain things outside yourself you will be happy, have love, and feel good about yourself. Isn't every ad campaign telling you that? This dynamic, however, never works to produce happiness, love, and self-esteem once you have decided you are Not OK. No amount of people telling you you are great makes you feel OK. You never get enough hugs, kisses, or toys to prove to your diminished sense of an unlovable self that you are loved. All these things on the outside are symbols for experiences that, in and of themselves, do not automatically create the corresponding internal experience. Thus you never get enough of what you don't really want.

Of course this *already existent conversation* you are born into and within which you are a victim doesn't go away when you achieve adult status! By that time you are so hooked into it that not only are you teaching it to your children, but are well harnessed to the treadmill yourself. Doesn't every ad promote happiness if you buy their product, vacation at their resort, lose weight, take up a certain activity, or ingest some pill? Sometimes you actually allow yourself to create the experience of happiness, but more often you followed their advice only to be disappointed.

At that point the evidence is staring us in the face, yet we never examine that the promise might be false. The promise is based on a false premise that an outside event (movie, vacation, sex, retirement, finding the right mate) or symbol (money, hugs, car, acknowledgement and praise) or substance (cigarettes, alcohol, drugs, food, or denial thereof) will **always** produce the promised experience. Instead we assume there must be something wrong with us, or we didn't get enough of the right stuff, or we didn't get the right stuff. Back on the treadmill we go again seeking **More** stuff, **Better** stuff, or **Different** stuff in the same old game of acquisition.

It should be emphasized that being *at effect* in relation to events, things, substances, other people, does not always produce negative experiences. Often we have positive experiences. And this of course sets the addictive hook even deeper. The observable truth is that **outside reality does not produce any experience at all**—we do! We have reactions to stimuli from the outside, but these reactions are a function of our prior conditioning. It is the false linkage between outside circumstance and inside experience that is so pervasive in our society and causes so much suffering. If the experience we happen to have is good (some form of pleasure), we become attached to that event, person, substance, or thing, only to experience pain when it or they go away.

On the other hand, if the experience is painful, we become attached in another way in trying to get rid of the thing that apparently caused the experience of pain. But in fact **there is no causal relationship between the outside world of form and symbol and one's inner experience** whether it be happiness and love or upset and anger. Unfortunately, the world we have been brought up in teaches us and daily reinforces just the opposite.

This is an extremely difficult "false cause" relationship to break as it is so pervasive in our society and forms the very core of this universal addiction into which we have all been entrained. If you make a list of the activities you do or stay away from, doesn't each have associated with it an experience you want or don't want? And don't you assume that if you do that activity you will have that experience - guaranteed? What about the food and substances you imbibe? Or the people who "make you feel good"?

This is not to say that **you** can't create a positive experience in those activities or by eating those foods or by being with those people. It is simply the mistaken idea that the activity, substance or person creates the experience for you, and you, as the *"at effect"* victim, are the beneficiary of that experience. This is what is meant by "false cause". People with more noticeable addictions like alcohol or drugs are just more hooked by the substance, but the mechanism is the same for all of us.

What follows is a small example from my own life. I have recently just kind of lost my taste for or interest in coffee probably because I changed my diet and stopped eating sugar. But before that occurred, I had looked forward to my morning latte because it tasted soooo good and gave me a energy boost I enjoyed, even though it seemed to exacerbate the arthritic pain I felt in my ankles. I would justify it by saying, "It's only one cup or the pain is worth the good feeling or maybe they aren't related."

Periodically I would stop drinking coffee to try and break the addictive habit. I would then feel like I was depriving myself, but stoically abstain until at some point the strong smell of freshly brewed coffee would over power my will and I would once again indulge. I even called it "America's legalized addiction"! In the grand scheme of things, coffee is probably not worth giving up, but for me this was indicative of so many other false cause relationships I had with activities, substance, people and places. It doesn't mean that I now don't do those activities, etc., it is that I am much more responsible for the experience I am creating and I know **I am creating it.**

There is one more important linkage we need to make, which relates to how we are creating our perceptive reality and the choice between being *at cause* or being *at effect*. You will recall that when we discussed perception, it was experientially verifiable that your actual visual experience of an object existed out where you experienced the object to be. The same is true with sound, which is located out in space, unless you are recalling a tune in your head which then is in your head. This means that your consciousness, and hence your essential self, not your body, is everywhere in your perceived reality. You might say that **who we are is the consciousness out of which all form arises.** This means that we are this vast multi-dimensional Being, creating our entire reality, and then because of an experience at or near birth, when our internal, inside-the-body experience was one of being abandoned and un-nurtured, we decided we really were alone and had to do it all ourselves. This is the birth of the ego.

It is important here to not make the ego wrong or bad. It is impossible not to have an ego and the ego is what relates to the outside agreement reality allowing us to get along in the world. Also you certainly need an ego before you can separate your Self from identifying with it! Unfortunately, along with this decision, "I am all alone," comes the experience, "I am at the effect of this big alien world out there and I had better learn how to survive in it." These experiences common to all of us have created the beliefs of the reality we now find ourselves in.

Declarations by creative, god-like beings such as we are, become the beliefs and sponsoring thoughts upon which reality is built. Once you consider yourself to be this little body in an alien world, the reptilian brain will cause that reality to survive. And the way it does that is to only see evidence or, if necessary, make up evidence which supports that view. That is why it is so difficult to help someone who is convinced he is a victim—advice on how he could pull himself out of the predicament **must** be rejected, as it implies that he might have had something to do with the predicament occurring in the first place.

On the other hand, the reptilian brain, which is causing the survival of who you consider yourself to be, can support your intentions to create a more positive reality when you choose to be *at cause.* Now it will allow you to start seeing how you actually created the reality you find yourself in, and once you discover how you created what you have, you can unwire it, and create something else. Finally, by taking responsibility for what you have already created, you will learn the dynamics and methodology for creating what you want. Thus every situation or circumstance has built within it the key to unlocking itself and the next step in your becoming an ever more powerful creator.

I believe that each of us has two purposes in common with all other beings. One is to learn how to consciously create reality, to own our power and learn how to create a positive reality with all other beings. The second is to learn how to be happy. In addition to those two, each of us has other lessons we are learning on the path to becoming more refined human beings. I trust this book will empower you to realize these purposes.

Before I talk about the steps of transformation, I want to emphasize that to BE in this moment of NOW and in each successive moment of NOW is all there is, ever was and ever will be. **This Is It.** Right here, right now. Perfect in its entirety. In which there is nothing for you to do and nowhere else you could be. This is the culmination of all your struggle, the future you have been waiting for. This is the way it turned out. And you are simply being present to this *way it is.*

However, to the mind, existing in and creating the illusion of time, it appears that there is something in the present that needs fixing and after it is fixed, which requires struggle and takes time, your life will be wonderful. This of course is a lie and a way of not being happy right now. The seven steps of transformation could easily fit into this paradigm—how to fix my life. So I am issuing a warning before going into this next part.

The key is to straddle this paradox rather than to fall into one side or the other—neither "Got to fix myself, struggle, struggle" nor "This is it, nothing matters, so why bother?" Buddha's recommendation was to take the middle road. To know that you are inherently OK, that you are already assured of winning the game because you are ultimately the source of the game (a child of God, if you like), and that you are the consciousness out of which this entire illusion is arising and passing away. At the same time, from your individualized perspective, persistently work away at becoming a more refined person and master of the game. This is the balance I would recommend, for it is only out of straddling the paradoxes that you will be able to be happy for all time.

CHAPTER SIX

The Seven Steps of Transformation

The word transformation attempts to distinguish between simply changing a pattern from one form to another and actually transmuting the energy of a pattern into a new way of being. For example, you could change partners and think you have really made a change, only to find the same patterns re-emerging with the new person—that would not be transformation.

Transformation would mean transmuting the energy of a pattern, through the state of no form (nothing), into a new form, a new pattern of behavior. A model of transformation is therefore useful in dealing with unwanted and dysfunctional patterns.

The following model of transformation is only an approximation of what I have found to be a flowing process. Sometimes the steps seemed to run together, happening rapidly and spontaneously. At other times, it has felt as though I was in the third step for years. To the extent that we are each in charge of our own evolution, these steps will give you certain milestones along your path and places to put your attention and intention.

1. RECOGNIZE

2. BE RESPONSIBLE

3. DISCOVER

4. LET GO/FORGIVE

5. DECLARE ANEW

6. PRACTICE/GET FEEDBACK

7. MASTER

1. RECOGNIZE

You can't deal with what you are not aware of. Given what you have learned about the reptilian brain's defense of your current reality, of the status quo, it is difficult to open yourself to new information or even a new way of holding old information. This is one of the benefits of your meditation/sitting practice and your constant efforts to see yourself in action: to be the witness to your thoughts, emotions, moods, physical sensations, and actions as you either review your day or are able to *be The Observer* in the course of living it.

I find this a continual practice of trying to stay awake to myself and over the years I have developed several physical reminders to help wake me up to each moment. My ongoing intention is to sharpen my focus and deepen my awareness for I know this is the tool of my evolution. I believe this is why there is so much emphasis in monasteries on mindfulness, for without awareness we are lost to ourselves in a quagmire of confusion and exterior forms.

The first awareness of some pattern in your life is its repetitive nature. "I have been here before." If you have the added feeling, "I am really sick and tired of this," so much the better as you will be motivated to do something about it. This first recognition is always from a position of you being *at effect* because that is the nature of all unconscious survival patterns. So it is important not to get discouraged by continually catching yourself in the role of a victim. If you can recognize that this is an opportunity for deepening insights about yourself and the nature of the reality you are creating and hence the key to being able to create more of what you want, then you will be holding the pattern in a useful way.

It is of utmost importance at this point to tell yourself the truth, to say exactly what is so. You will find that you can always deal with the truth, no matter how uncomfortable, but a lie only keeps things confused and persisting because a lie is a way of resisting the truth. Part of mindfulness is to become a courageous truth teller.

2. BE RESPONSIBLE

This step involves the conscious choice to be *at cause,* to take an "I am willing to take the mental position that I am causing this pattern in its entirety, even though I don't see at the moment how I am causing it." Most often you will not immediately see any new information as to how you have created things to be the way they are. However, the important thing about mentally saying this to yourself is that you start to readjust the filters that the reptilian brain uses to cause realities to persist.

While the reptilian brain is an automatic survival mechanism, it is causing the survival of who you, the being, consider yourself to be. So by changing your mental stance to one of responsibility *(at cause)*, you allow new information to get through the filters that will show you how you created the pattern of which you are now aware.

A key here is willingness—the willingness to take the stand of, "I am responsible, even when I don't see how yet." It also helps to ask others what they see, and even though they might be defending their position that they have nothing to do with what's happening, often they are only too anxious to point out your culpability! Hopefully you will experience this as helpful and thank them for the feedback. It takes some practice to get through the fear of rejection and embarrassment of doing this, but after all, courage is action in the face of fear, so you are developing courage in yourself as well.

3. DISCOVER

The discovery step continues for as long as it takes for you to observe and re-experience how you created this pattern and the interlocking web of beliefs which make up your reality. I have found that I will often get an insight which frees up some part of the pattern, but that the rest may take years to unravel. So this often resembles simply sitting within the pattern, waking up my observer self, and seeing what I see. Often you can learn a lot after the fact by reviewing things that have happened during the day, attempting always to ask the question "How did I create that?" A journal can help here if you write your observations down in a kind of free flow approach.

Trying to figure it out, as opposed to simply observing it, doesn't tend to help, as most of what you are thinking about is your own justifications for why things are the way they are and come from the pattern itself. You need to observe the mind, not be in it. Remember, the reptilian brain has not given up its valiant struggle to keep the old reality intact. To the contrary it will often fight back even harder the closer you get to the truth. The truth sets you free as the integrity of that pattern is destroyed and its automatic survival-oriented hold over you is released, but the ego does not see it that way!

As you spend more time being aware of the pattern, you can often catch yourself in the middle of it and stop or change the automatic response that would have led to the same old result. This is a particularly embarrassing moment as you catch yourself and need to stop, apologize, and take new action when the natural tendency is to want to justify your actions, make yourself right and the other person or circumstance wrong. This desire to make yourself right is a very strong survival tool and must be overcome in order to break the pattern. In a sense you have to make a choice: "Do I want to be right or alive?" It is not without some evidence that the expression "dead right" came about!

At some point, you will be so aware of the pattern that you will start to notice it arising within yourself. You will start to observe the emotions and be able to experience them without having to express them through words or actions. You will then start to see the beliefs out of which the emotions come. At about this point, you will be aware of what triggers the pattern and even perhaps know how you set up the conditions for those triggers to exist. When you finally see the sponsoring thought, in the form of a decision or declaration you made, the whole pattern will lift and you, your Self, will no longer be trapped in it.

If you are very mindful and aware, the discovery step can and will occur in the process of your daily living. You will be going through the pattern in a conscious way, gradually extracting your Self from it. But often we are confronted with unwanted patterns of conditioned behavior, emotions and thoughts, which are so overwhelming that we need a more focused approach for discovering how the patterns are structured and held together. The following Discovery Process is designed to allow you to observe a pattern in a little more organized fashion.

EXERCISE 9

Discovery Process*

(one hour or more)

Read this exercise through to get an idea of the sequence and then do it with your eyes closed. Alternatively, have a friend read the instructions as you do the process on some issue in your life. Your friend's job is to read the instructions aloud and not to give any advice or make comments on what you say, as an important part of doing this process successfully is to take whatever it is you get in response to the instructions. To observe whatever you see, sense or feel, without judging or assessing it as "right" or "wrong."

Start with an issue or problem in your life that you would like to disappear. Next you must define an aspect of the problem you are actually experiencing or could experience and would know when it went away. This we will define as your *item*. For example: Let's suppose the problem is, "My relationship with my son. We always end up arguing and he never seems to listen to me or want my advice." Now as real as this might seem to you, the above, as stated, cannot be worked on very well as it is too conceptual and not experiential enough.

*This exercise, originally designated "The Truth Process," was included in the *est* Training and is reprinted with the permission of Landmark Education, LLC. All rights reserved.

Using this example, you would ask yourself, "What exactly do I experience when my son and I get into an argument?" Using your power to observe, you might come up with: "my anger at my son" or "my sadness over the state of our relationship" or even more specific "a four inch wide band of tightness across my chest." The more experientially specific you can be in identifying your *item* the better the process will work. Also it must be something *you* experience directly, not what you do or what happens to others.

Next close your eyes, and spend a few moments scanning your body internally with your consciousness to let go of any tensions you have. Relax. Now repeat the *item* to yourself "my sadness..." or "the four inch band...", or your friend can repeat the *item* with each of the following instructions. You need to keep repeating the item to yourself throughout the process to stay focused on one item at a time, and keep the mind bringing up only what is associated with that item. In terms of the model of the mind, your intention is to move back down the string of images that make up this pattern to its source, observing each experience as it surfaces.

Repeat the item. Are you willing to let go of the item? If the answer is no, work on something else. You are not yet ready to give this up. Perhaps the payoff, what you get out of having it, is still too great. Work on something else for now until you can get a definite "Yes" to that question.

Repeat the item to yourself. Locate and describe a body sensation associated with the item. Locate another sensation and describe it, and another, and another until you have observed all that you are aware of. If you drift off, repeat the item to yourself and then take what you get in response to the question. Describe each sensation in terms of its location, size, shape, and the sensation itself e.g. "A two-inch diameter ball-shaped painful pressure one inch below the sternum."

Repeat the item to yourself and observe the emotions and feelings you have associated with the item. Ask, "What emotions and feelings do I have associated with the item?" Take whatever you see, sense or feel and allow yourself to experience and go through the emotion while at the same time keeping your observer consciousness present. What other emotions do you experience associated with the item? Keep asking the question until you no longer experience a new emotion. You are in the process of taking an inventory of every aspect of experience associated with the item.

Next, repeat the item to yourself and observe the thoughts you have about it. What other thoughts do you have? What opinions? What judgments? What things have others said (friends, doctors, etc)? What things have you read about the item? What decisions have you made about the item? Inventory your entire current mental realm: all thoughts, ideas, opinions, judgments, things others have said, attitudes, conclusions, decisions.

Now repeat the item to yourself and locate an image from the past associated with the item. Take whatever you see, sense or feel in response to the instruction. If it is darkness, describe the darkness. If it is a general feeling of pressure, describe that feeling. When you have an incident from the past (a memory) in mind, start at the beginning of the incident and go through it to the end, describing what happened. "He did this, I said that, she did......." As objectively as possible, describe what happened. Also allow yourself to experience whatever emotions are there in the incident.

After you have gone through the incident once, go back to the beginning and go through it one more time, describing what happened, noticing if you missed anything. After observing that incident thoroughly from beginning to end, look to see if you made any decisions about yourself, other people, or the world at that time. If you experience an energy release, in that you have seen something you had not previously seen, and the pattern seems to have lifted, you might not need to go back any further. Check to see if the item has disappeared. If "Yes", open your eyes. You are finished for now. If "No", continue.

Repeat the item to yourself and locate an earlier similar incident from your past associated with the item. Again, take whatever you get and describe what you see, sense, or feel. Go through the incident describing what happened and then go back a second time describing what happened. Let yourself experience the emotions and feelings. Keep your Observer on, staying present, while you are reliving these past incidents. What decisions did you make about yourself, others, and the world in which you live? If you get a release, stop. If not, continue ....

Repeat the item to yourself and locate a yet earlier similar incident from your past associated with the item. Take what you get. How old are you? What happened? What decisions did you make if any? Keep going back until you get a release or run out of time.

A couple of comments: If you do not get a release during any single session, you will still get value out of the process as any time you observe your experience you are in the process of clearing it up and releasing yourself and your energy from being trapped within the pattern. Observing the mind is like peeling an onion from the outside, only to reveal another layer underneath. Sometimes, having not reached the bottom of a pattern in a particular session, you may be more in touch with various aspects of the pattern than you were when you started—experiencing emotions of sadness or anger or feelings of depression, agitation, low self-esteem, and so on.

These feeling have always been a part of that pattern, stored in your mind/body and are now simply coming to the surface of your awareness. If you keep your observer on and continue to stay awake to your experience, these feelings will disappear in the process of you observing them. To do this, it is important to let them simply be the way they are without trying to change them in any way. If you try to change them, suppress them or resist them, they will persist.

Second, in doing the above process, you will never get more than you are able to handle. That doesn't mean that you won't experience intense emotions and relive old wounds, only that what you experience has been inside you, suppressed and unconscious to be sure, but nonetheless totally active in replaying the automatic pattern and thereby running your life. You have said that you are willing to let the pattern go and by implication you are willing to look at its essential nature. You will therefore get the pattern in doses that you are capable of handling. If you somehow are not up to handling a portion of the pattern yet, the unconsciousness will put you to sleep or just shroud the key incident until the intensity of your observation can penetrate the unconsciousness. The only way out of these patterns is to go through them consciously.

Lucy's Process

Here is a real example. A workshop participant whom I will call Lucy complained of always being afraid that her son was going to die. Since the birth of her son more than twenty years ago, Lucy had nightly heart palpitations, often had paralyzing symptoms of fear and was constantly worried about her son's health and wellbeing. She was in a state of high agitation at the time of the workshop as her son had recently moved away from home and her inability to constantly know his state of health seemed to have made the pattern worse. She was taking medication to calm her down and sleeping pills to get through the night.

She agreed to work on the pattern as part of a demonstration of how the *Discovery Process* works. I told her she would need to select an item that she was definitely experiencing when she was in a high state of worry about her son's death and that she would know had disappeared if and when it did. After some discussion, she chose a two-inch-wide pain across the front of her chest. She had a long list of other body sensations associated with the band of pain across her chest. These included tension in the forehead from one temple to another, a pain and tightness in the back of the throat, tension in her thighs, and a burning pressure the size of a grapefruit below the sternum. I just kept asking her "What other body sensations do you experience associated with the band of pain across your chest?" When there were no more she could find, we went on to emotions and feeling.

She let herself experience and was aware of sadness, fear, and a kind of helplessness all associated with her item. This took a while as an emotion would come up and she would allow herself to experience it and then we would go on to the next.

She got in touch with many thoughts, ideas, and decisions that she had made in the course of the twenty years since her son's birth. Perhaps the most prevailing theme was her helplessness. She was tortured by what seemed irreconcilable thoughts. If she worried about him was she somehow drawing that reality toward her, in the sense of what many metaphysical teachings say, "You get what you focus on"? But how could she not worry? If she didn't pay attention and do everything in her power to prevent it, he might die. This left her paralyzed, feeling helpless, and agitated. Also she felt like a bad mother somehow. She could never do enough to feel at peace. What if this was his last day and she hadn't done everything she could? She would imagine how terrible she would feel about herself. During all of this talking by Lucy, I was simply listening, acknowledging that I heard what she said, and asking the next question, "What other thoughts, ideas, opinions or conclusions do you have associated with the band of pain across your chest?" I was making no other comment about what she was saying.

As we started getting into images from the past associated with her item, Lucy first went to an incident in which her son had a collapsed lung and almost died. This happened about the same time as she and her husband were getting a divorce. At this point I kept her on track by simply saying, "Associated with the pain across your chest, locate an earlier similar incident."

It would have been easy for the mind to get sidetracked on the whole divorce thing with her husband. She saw an earlier incident where she sent her son to camp, at her husband's request and against her own instincts, and her son was in pain all summer.

Next she went to the time of her son's birth, to the worry she had while she was carrying him and the fact that he almost did die of some rare blood disease. In this incident, doctors screwed up. It had been hard to find people to give blood for the transfusion and a long list of difficulties and problems persisted for the next year. There was lots of drama and tears in the retelling of this incident, and when Lucy would start repeating herself, I would only ask "Is there something you haven't told us about this incident?" Having recounted this traumatic incident, I asked whether the band of pain across her chest had cleared up. Upon looking, Lucy responded, "No." So on we went.

"Locate an earlier similar incident associated with...." "I'm a little girl in my house." "How old are you?" "About six." "What's happening? Describe whatever you see, sense or feel." Lucy described the childhood fear she had that her mother was going to die. How her mother was rather frail, and often sick. How her father was not home much and at times raging and abusive when he was. How Lucy did everything she could to take care of her mother and not offend her father, so he wouldn't get mad at her. She had decided at about this time that she was pretty much on her own in the world and that there weren't many people out there to give her love. It was a kind of "poor me" story. Still the pain across her chest was present, although greatly reduced.

Once again I asked the question to locate an earlier similar incident associated with the pain across her chest. This time Lucy took a long time to respond. So I said "What are you experiencing?" And she said, "I'm in a tube and it's just kind of dark." "What are you feeling?" "It feels tight all over and I can't move. Oh, I'm trying to be born, but I'm stuck. I feel helpless and the band of tightness around my chest is intense and my throat is so tight and closed I can't breathe. I'm trying to move my legs but I can't."

As she explored further, Lucy discovered that she had decided that she was worthless, unlovable, and helpless. This declaration then formed the underpinnings, the sponsoring thought, of her reality for the next 50 years. At this point the band of pain was gone so we stopped.

As she pieced it together after opening her eyes, Lucy could see that her Not OKness (sense of being worthless, unlovable, and helpless) had been the motivation behind a life of constantly proving she was better than men in similar positions. She was an extremely successful division manager of a company, but experientially it was never enough or it was dissatisfying, and she always had to do it all by herself. With her family and friends, she was driven to do things for them, going overboard to get and sustain their acceptance and love. She had proven herself far from helpless by anyone's standard, but it never quite produced the sense of satisfaction and OKness she was looking for.

The other aspect was her addiction to feeling worthless, unloved and unlovable, helpless and paralyzed. She would imagine her son's sickness and possible death, convinced that she didn't deserve him and that's why something would happen to him, while at the same time struggling within herself to not have these thoughts. This fantasy took her out of present time into her head (worrying), yet at the same time produced the experience of feeling miserable in the present moment.

At the end of that session she was able to admit that the truth at any moment was that her son was either alive or dead. That is the way it is and always will be. She saw that her addiction to worry constantly took her out of the present moment and thus out of life and into her own private world of suffering. She committed to letting go of this pattern and felt confident that she could live with the truth of the way things are. After the seminar she reported having the best week of sleep that she could ever remember, peaceful and relaxed.

In seeing her decision to have to do everything on her own, to be strong, always in control, and so forth, she recognized how much it had cost her in terms of the love and support she experienced in her marriage, at work, and in her circle of friends. She committed to asking for help at work and accepting and letting in more of the love that came from her friends. She chose to declare a new way of being, "I am loving and lovable, generous, whole and enough, living in an abundant world, fulfilled, happy and at peace."

LESSONS FROM LUCY

Lucy's case has all the elements I wish to emphasize. First, at very early and formative ages each of us makes decisions in the category of "I am Not OK. " And these decisions, along with the feelings that accompanied them, are stored in the mind as necessary to survival. Second, these decisions/declarations get reinforced through what the reptilian survival brain considers as similar incidents later on in life. These start to form the pattern, which becomes the basis for the automatic behaviors triggered every time something in the current environment is similar enough to be considered a threat to survival. This is called being upset.

Lucy's worry/anxiety pattern was one of these constant upsets that had in it all of the body sensations, emotions, thoughts, attitudes, and decisions from the past. Since these body sensations and emotions are replays of the earlier sensations and emotions, it is possible to use them (your item) to follow the chain of images backwards to the original source of the pattern.

Third, the Not OKness that has moved to a subconscious level you are now **sure** is true about you, rather than being aware that it is an erroneous decision made by a young, semi-conscious child. This Not OKness becomes the motivation for a personality formation that sets about trying to prove just the opposite, "I really am OK." Of course, many of the traits of this personality are picked up from your mother and father since they are the available role models. In addition, it looks to the child that if you are sufficiently like your parents you will get the unconditional love and acceptance you so desperately crave. But the main reason that this personality and its accomplishments remain unsatisfying is that no amount of outside symbols of love and success can give you the experience of being loved and successful when you have already decided that you are flawed, unlovable, and worthless.

Fourth is the addiction to the negative experience of Not OKness. When we so often say we want happiness, it seems strange that we are so inept at creating it. Yet an understanding of the nature of the reptilian brain causing the survival of who you consider yourself to be provides the needed insight into our own human mechanism. Once you consider yourself to be Not OK, the reptilian brain must keep replaying that experience, with all of its feelings of worthlessness, over and over again in order to assure survival. Lucy not only replayed all of the horrible feelings nightly, but she maintained a victim stance to that which she was creating.

This is another aspect of the addiction which keeps you from actually observing what is going on. After all, if I am a victim, the best I can do is learn to deal with the pattern, through drugs, compulsive behaviors or distractions, but never to "disappear" it which requires an *at cause* stance and a willingness to look at and observe the truth. None of which the ego is prone to do.

CASSANDRA'S TALE

Cassandra, a woman in one of my workshops, went back through her life of physical abuse by a drunk husband, to physical abuse by a drunk father at the age of six, to being told she was "good for nothing" around age three, to being unwanted in the womb and then unwanted because she was a girl at birth. At least that was her interpretation and what she had held onto throughout her life. There were many tears and lots of anger at the abusive men in her life as she finally saw where she had first experienced the feelings of being unwanted and worthless, "good for nothing".

However, as she sat there, it was obvious Cassandra was still stuck in the pattern and experiencing none of the relief which usually accompanies such deep realizations. She now knew where it all had come from and could see how she had spent her life proving she was worthwhile through helping others (she was a therapist) and through her many accomplishments. But this did not give her the sense of self-love and self-worth she desired.

When I suggested it was because she had not owned the fact that she had decided she was worthless and Not OK and that she was still holding herself as a victim in her own life story, she said her whole being cried out, "No, it was them!" She had spent her whole life proving she was OK. How could she have been the one who actually decided and declared the opposite and was thus responsible for the 54 years of struggle and anguish she had been through? It was only by finally seeing that she agreed with her parents, by determining for herself the answer to the questions, "Why don't they want me?" and "What does this mean about me?" that Cassandra was finally free of the pattern.

While all the evidence for what Cassandra's mother and father were really thinking and feeling as she was being born were part of the multi-sensory total records of that incident, Cassandra never was aware of them and thus made up her own (baby's) mind about what it all meant. In that time of feeling all alone and helpless, she also felt and decided she was *at the effect* of this larger reality out there that she had to somehow appease and cajole into giving her what she needed and wanted. This decision, again in the form of a declaration by her, the creator of her reality, establishes her in a victim role in the very reality she was unknowingly creating.

Until Cassandra was willing to admit that she was the source of her reality, as disastrous as her life drama had been and as much as she wanted to still blame them and be right about everything they had done to her, she was not free. Until you observe and own that it is you who are doing all this to yourself, by the original declaration, "I am Not OK," and the subsequent declarations/decisions on top of that which form the sponsoring thoughts of your reality, you will not be free either.

I trust that by knowing where generally to look, you will be assisted in efficiently getting to the bottom of the patterns you wish to transform. The heart of the matter will always be some form of, "I am Not OK". You will need to discover what your particular version of that is. In addition, you will need to know how you then went about constructing your exterior persona, your act. This is as varied as there are people, but the structure will always be the same. Each of us is a personality trying to prove that "I am OK," driven by the opposite and living in a world which itself is insufficient, flawed and not OK. We are all trapped in this creation until we can observe it, see it for what it is, and move onto something more loving and productive.

As I have learned more about myself, I have seen that my own inner insecurity (my not-good-enough, flawed nature) has not only driven an exterior personality that has overcompensated with accomplishments and knowledge, but has also through my perceptive mechanism, projected a flawed not-good-enough nature onto others so I could fix them or outshine them. This, one more time, proves to my ego's gratification that I was better than them. My mind's script then reads, "They will now give me the love I want."

This strategy never worked out, since I was basically communicating to them through word and example that they were Not OK, and who appreciates that experience? You would think that I would have awakened to this false premise long ago, but as my ego was being stroked by admiration and applause (substitutes for love), I had little incentive for waking up. That was until people started leaving me and I started observing the dynamics of this pattern.

Another indicator of the form of your own "Not OKness" is to observe how you judge others to be. We live in a reflective universe which reflects back our deepest beliefs about ourselves because the world we live in arose out of the same decision that forms the basis of who we consider ourselves to be. These judgments are almost always statements about our deepest fears about ourselves projected onto another, both as a way of keeping our distance as well as a way to reinforce our ego's "better than" stance. I used to notice my own mind making derogatory comments about people as I would pass them in an airport. "Fat", "nigger", "ugly" would resound in my head and only when I put some attention on myself did I realize I was feeling very vulnerable and insecure at that moment, which in turn came from my own basic feeling of worthlessness. Here in the airport, I didn't have my teacher role to play and wasn't getting approval from my students. Here I was naked. So you see, if you keep your watcher on, even a crowded airport can instruct you about what you are creating.

It is extremely useful, having seen the "Not OKness" out of which you created your reality, to go back through your life and retell your story from the point of view that you caused what occurred. It is helpful to say, "How I got them to do it to me was…….." remembering that non-actions or allowing things to happen is a way of creating that is as powerful as actions themselves. It is also useful to see how your attitudes, your body postures and body language, as well as your projections and your beliefs of how things are or have to be all create your reality.

By doing this you will be confirming how powerful you are and therefore how powerful you can be in creating what you now desire. We all live within a story, an interpretation of the many things that are occurring, so it is important to consciously reconstruct your story. It will then become the backdrop of your current creation. If it is a victim's story you live within, then it will have all the experiences that go along with that point of view. If it is an "I am *at cause*" story it will have all the possibility for you co-creating with all other aspects of your reality what you want.

EXERCISE 10:

My *at Cause* Story

(one to two hours or more)

In your notebook write your life story from the point of view that you caused all the events to happen. You need to keep the actual events accurate, but you can use other evidence to prove your new **at cause** stance. It is especially important to re-write all those incidents you have always related to as a victim. The stories that when you retell them elicit sympathy from others. You can help prompt your mind with, "How I got them to do it to me was..."

To know thyself has always been the key to power in the world. To see clearly both the functional as well as dysfunctional patterns in your life, and to own them, so that you do not have to automatically operate out of them, but can consciously choose every moment; this is both freedom and power. The step of *Discovery* leads to wisdom as you gain these insights into yourself.

4. LET GO/FORGIVE

Often at the end of a powerful *Discovery Process* such as Lucy had, there is a huge release of energy and a number of insights about the nature of the pattern and the reality you created. This energy is now available for the creation of a new reality and is most often experienced as flowing, free energy, and the experience of aliveness. People often ride for weeks on the energy and insights released, effortlessly producing many of the things they have always wanted.

The three-cycle nature of the world in which we live is create, persist, and destroy. Things are created (energy into matter), persist awhile, and then disappear, releasing the energy held in place and making way for the new. To stop resisting life, by telling the truth about and observing your experience, puts you back into that creative energy flow.

Before you can let go of something, you have to first have it. This means not only taking an *at cause* ownership stance about any given pattern, but also you must fully stop resisting it. Most people are either denying or actively resisting what they don't want in their lives. This is not only the source of the pattern's persistence, but also the source of the entire struggle to get rid of it and the suffering which having it, but trying not to, brings. To embrace your shadow self, these negative aspects of yourself, is none other than the process of fully owning what you have. Once you fully have it, you can let it go.

Letting go of a pattern is more like LETTING IT BE. There is nothing you have to do. In fact it is important to literally <u>do</u>

nothing. To let something be is to fully accept it the way it is. Anything that you can let be, will let you be, and it is the pure, unencumbered Being that is necessary for the next step. This process is as if you are shifting from being totally identified with your ego's patterns and more and more identified with your Observer Self. It is the actor recovering herself, realizing she is not the role.

Of course, it is not as easy as it sounds. Most people want to hang onto their past, as it gives them a sense of identity. To the ego, letting go of past patterns and those old familiar roles looks like annihilation. Therefore, the **willingness** to accept things the way they are, to let it be OK that you are experiencing your ego feeling Not OK when that is so, is an important aspect of this step.

In the process of taking responsibility, of being willing to take an *at cause* stance, for the reality in which you find yourself, people often interpret this as meaning, "It's my fault and I am to blame." First, being *at cause* for something that didn't work implies no blame or wrongdoing nor the subsequent necessity to feel badly or punish yourself. It is a willingness to see your causal relationship to the events and circumstances of your life in a simple and direct way. "Oh, I did this or did not do that and the result was X. Now that I see what happened, I can try a different strategy and see what the result of that will be." This is a far cry from the "Mea culpa" with the accompanying gnashing of teeth and self-flagellation which normally takes place.

This brings us to a conversation about GUILT. Guilt is one of the true insanities of humankind. To understand this, imagine a completely natural system in which a felt need is responded to by an action, which in turn either works to satisfy the need or doesn't work. In this natural system if something works, the action is reinforced and repeated. If, on the other hand, the action does not work, a correction is tried until an action is found which does work. This action is repeated until it no longer works and then changed.

The schematic of a natural system would look like this:

NATURAL SYSTEM

Imagine a bear coming out of a winter of hibernation. The felt need is hunger. Now the bear remembers from previous years that grubs, a favorite treat, can be found under dead logs. So he rolls over a log and finds either grubs or no grubs. If he finds grubs he will keep rolling over logs until that felt need is satiated. If he doesn't find grubs, he will wander down to the stream to see if the salmon are running, or on to the berry patch, if there are no fish. He is just a bear operating in a natural system.

What about humans? Humans certainly have felt needs, and take actions that produce similar works/doesn't work outcomes. However, because of our conditioning and the conversation into which we are born, we don't leave it at that. We immediately **label** the natural consequences of our actions and take it into a realm of psychological insanity. When something doesn't work, we label it a failure and immediately know from our upbringing in school and at home that only bad little girls and boys have failures. And bad people get what they deserve, which is punishment. As a child, punishment took the form of withdrawal of love and affection, rejection (go to your room), or sometimes physical and emotional abuse.

This dynamic was repeated hundreds of times at home and in school to entrain us, so that even now we immediately think that doing something which doesn't work is a failure and deserves punishment. The first two in the sequence (doesn't work result, failure, I am bad, punishment) are linked in our minds not as an external fact and its corresponding label, but as one and the same thing. By association, if I have failures, I must be a failure. And since there are no parents around to punish me, I had better punish myself by feeling ashamed and Not OK; in other words, guilty.

To understand the dynamics of guilt, we only have to return to our addiction to feeling Not OK. Once we have decided that we are Not OK the greatest form of punishment is rejection and the withdrawal of love, as it returns us immediately to all those bad feelings of abandonment and shame (the helplessness, the worthlessness, the hurt and anger, the panic, "I'm going to die", and so on) that accompany the Not OKness. As far back as there are records, adults have used the fear of rejection as a way of getting children to comply with the already existent conversation, the normative set of beliefs, which they, the adults, are promoting and defending as necessary to their own ego's survival. Thus the patterns are passed down from generation to generation.

Guilt is a false emotion in that it is entirely societally based and learned as part of the conversation into which we were born. As adults, we justify this self-flagellation and self-punishment as necessary to learn the lesson; "If I beat myself up enough I won't forget and do something so stupid again". We also have it connected to caring: "If I do something which doesn't work and don't beat myself up by feeling really guilty, I didn't really care". Why isn't the belief "I will feel good about myself for what I am learning and try a different strategy next time?"

Guilt has another payoff for the ego. It allows you to maintain the image of yourself as a good person, because only a good person would feel badly about himself and punish himself when he did something bad (didn't work = failure = bad). If a bad person did the same thing, he would just say, "Oh well, what did you expect?" People often remain in a constant state of guilt by creating expectations for themselves that they never meet. The expectations help support an internal image of "what a wonderful, productive person I am" which is all part of the proving I'm OK act. The never meeting the expectations and feeling guilty keeps the Not OKness part of the ego intact.

Imagine Mr. Bear coming out of his cave, hungry. He goes over to a log and rolls it over, only to find there are no grubs. He then proceeds to start beating himself around the head and shoulders muttering something which sounds like, "Bad bear, bad bear, bad, bad." Now you would say there is one insane bear, while in humans that conditioned nonsense is accepted as normal!!!

Unfortunately the success side is just as insane. Doing something that worked was immediately labeled a success, and those who had successes were good little girls and boys, who got rewards (hugs, food, attention and privileges). In and of itself, the rewards don't seem dysfunctional. The problem is tying an action that worked and its natural consequences to additional rewards that are psychologically-based (acceptance or rejection). This overlay of conditional love by parents and adults when we are growing up means we have entrained ourselves into a fear-based form of manipulation, which we perpetuate on ourselves and others. Every frantic effort to accomplish is driven by this fear, and everyone soon learns that when you make a mistake, rewards will be replaced with punishment and the goodies of life will disappear.

Schematically:

To counteract our conditioning and our tendency to beat up on ourselves when we do something that doesn't work, which, by the way, justifies our beating up on others for their mistakes, we need to practice FORGIVENESS.

As you understand your own human dynamics more intimately, you will begin to understand how other people are driven by their own low self-esteem to do the things they do. With this understanding comes compassion as you realize they too are suffering, and with compassion comes forgiveness. Forgiving others helps release the resentments and angers which erode your happiness and wellbeing and do little to actually get the other person to change. So practice forgiving others; it works.

The second realm of forgiveness is to say, "I am sorry" and to ask forgiveness from others. Usually this will include some form of commitment to not do the hurtful action again. It is ultimately true that the other person is creating his or her own response, as in feeling hurt and angry, so at some level, there is nothing to forgive. However, if you knew that what you were going to do or say was going to trigger hurt in the other, then why would you do it?

Often some of our communication is unintentionally hurtful or just plain unskillful application, even when justified by, "I'm only trying to help." When the underlying message is "You're not OK or you are not as good as me," it is hurtful to anyone who has not fully cleared up his core issue of "Not OKness." So not only does saying "I'm sorry" help with others, but it is especially important in your battle with your own ego, as each time you say, "I'm sorry," you reassert your Self. The other person may not accept your act of contrition, but you will know you have tried, and as a result, respect yourself more.

The third realm of forgiveness is learning to forgive and accept yourself. We tend to treat ourselves worse than we treat others, which in turn justifies our maltreatment of others. Forgiving yourself and the willingness to accept yourself as you are in this moment, warts and all, is one of the major practices required to end the pattern of punishing yourself for mistakes.

After all, how can you learn to master the game of life without making mistakes? Given the information at hand and the choices you saw then as a function of your survival patterns, haven't you always tried to do your best? You might see different choices now, but you needed that experience then to finally see and come to grips with the pattern.

When you see the perfection of this evolutionary process we are in, when you understand that everything you went through was necessary for where you are now, and when you love where you are now, you will welcome the next pattern you get in touch with, no matter how painful. Because through that door lies your next level of true freedom.

The more you can let yourself just be the way you are, without judging yourself, beating yourself up, and trying to not be the way you are, the faster you will get through the patterns and old dysfunctional programming from your past and step into the realm of true freedom. As you accept yourself more and more, you will be creating the foundation for happiness, for happiness is a function of accepting things the way they are.

5. DECLARE ANEW

Having cleared the space by letting go of an old way of Being, the actions and results which automatically flowed from that way of Being will also start to disappear. At this point, you have started to get on top of the pattern so that you have it, rather than it having you. While there may still be some momentum to the old habitual behaviors and some confusion and uncertainty about what behaviors will replace them, there is, nevertheless, space for the new.

It is now possible to declare a new way of being. You already know how to do this, as you have been living out of your declared reality all your life. This time, however, you will be doing it consciously. Each aspect that was done unconsciously will now be done consciously. All realities start in the realm of thought and are made real through word and action. "In the beginning was the word" is very practical advice on reality creation.

The most powerful form of declaration I have found is one that starts with "I am." This is a statement of being *at cause* for what is to follow. It is the way it is, solely because I say so. When initiating a new reality, this seems a very brash thing to say as the evidence for the reality's existence is so minimal. You must remember that the evidence in a BE -> DO -> HAVE reality creation process comes in the Have stage, not during the initiation. So making a statement, "I am a loving and lovable person," when up until now the evidence would point to just the opposite, seems the height of arrogance and fantasy.

This is the aspect of ourselves that we have rarely experienced previously—being the conscious creator. In the past, the declaration "I am unlovable" came in reaction to a particular circumstance and the feeling you were abandoned. And since the conversation you were born into included a lot of "unlovable" people (certainly your parents among them) trying to prove they were worthy of being loved, the pattern was well known and all you had to do was learn it from them.

The process of conscious creation is quite different because there are few precedents and almost no evidence for the new reality. In addition, you have to create new behaviors consistent with your newly declared way of Being and this feels strange and awkward as you first try them out.

It is as though you have been playing one role your whole life, such as how to manipulate others to give you love and attention by being a victim, and now you are going to play a different role in the same general play. The other part is that you have trained all the other actors to act a certain way, which supports your victim role, and at this point they have a vested interest in keeping things the way they have always been! So it is a bit scary to declare, "I am happy. I am responsible for what is occurring in my life and I will actively change what doesn't work. I am deserving of love. I am sufficient and live in an abundant world that supports me."

Affirmations in the form of declarations will only work when you have cleared away what was previously in the space through your power of observation. If you try to make affirmations without doing the preliminary work, they will only reinforce your sense of Not OKness (There must be something wrong with me, I am a failure) as you continue to say them and they don't work. How could the affirmations work? There is no space into which they can manifest.

This does not mean that INTENTION and VISION are not important. Having an intention to make something occur and a vision of what it will be like when it does occur are both very important aspects of the creation process. Against the background of intention and vision, you will see what doesn't work and therefore what you need to transform using the first four steps of this transformation process. Also, going through the process of getting clear about what you want in your life and then focusing your DESIRE on its attainment provides the motivation to do the actual work of transformation.

It is important to recognize that the creation process is neither too laissez faire nor too effortful. Effort implies that you have to overcome something and if you have cleared the space by eliminating the old, there is literally nothing to overcome, since you are creating out of nothing into emptiness. So, if you find yourself thinking, "I really need to work hard at this," it must be because there is still some aspect of who you consider yourself to be which is undeserving and Not OK.

Much of what we do see created in our world (some of which is actually the rearrangement of already existent elements and not true creation at all) is produced with a great deal of effort. However, the pure process of creation itself only requires focused attention in a relaxed and confident manner. It does not actually require effort. It is as if I declare, "I am happy or I am loving," then I let it go and continue through the day doing what a happy/loving person might do and noticing evidence which confirms my happy/loving nature.

The idea of focused attention is important because it is a skill you can develop and which has big payoffs over time. There is an old saying in the metaphysical movement: "You get what you focus on." Now it is also true that in order to bring things into the physical realm, you have to maintain a consistent focus over a period of time. Often people bounce around from one thing they want to something else, never building their focused attention to a high enough intensity or over a long enough time to actually bring much into existence. This is also why people seem to get what they most fear, or what they resist, because in a reverse sort of way they are focusing their attention for some time on what they fear.

EXERCISE 11

My Vision

(two hours or more)

In your notebook, write your vision for your preferred future. Describe it in as much detail as possible and cover all aspects of your life: work, family, community, relationships, recreation, vacations, financial status, hobbies, where you live. Spend whatever time is necessary refining this vision until it accurately describes what you really desire.

Next describe yourself. What is the profile of the person who would live in this reality?

Finally, out of that vision and description of yourself, formulate a series of declarations about yourself and your world that would be the sponsoring thoughts for that reality. These should be fairly condensed so that you can remember them and say them from time to time during your day.

EXERCISE 12

Practicing Declaration

(10 minutes per session)

With a list of these declarations in hand, stand in front of a mirror (do this in private) and look down at your list until you have one declaration in mind and then look up into the mirror and say the declaration out loud, looking yourself in the eye. Repeat this as many times as is necessary, perhaps over several days, until you can say it without effort and without your mind bringing up all the evidence for why the statement isn't true. In other words, say it until you are simply being there with the declaration.

EXERCISE 13

Creating a Visual Image of your Vision

(one to two hours)

Another aspect of this exercise is to create a collage of images representing your vision/desired future. Put this collage up in a place that you pass from time to time during the day, like in the hall on the way to the bathroom. On several occasions daily, stop in front of your collage and just be there with it, for 30 seconds or so, not thinking, not planning how to get it, not wanting it strongly, not investing your happiness in this possible future; just being with it in as neutral a way as possible and letting go of any thoughts that arise. Then go on with your day.

The ability to be with what you desire in a non-attached way will give you the greatest chance of having what you want. To assist you in becoming non-attached to what you desire, it is useful to determine two or more outcomes with which you would be equally satisfied. This will help you to be more open and receptive to miraculous contributions from the rest of your universe.

6. PRACTICE/FEEDBACK

Only by practicing a new skill or a new role in a play do we learn and finally master it. Furthermore, learning takes place best in an environment-rich in feedback. The classic example is learning how to ride a bike. Although this is a very complex motor skill involving many different muscles, almost all of us learned how to do it in a relatively short time. You practiced of course, but you were also in an environment of constant feedback—gravity. Gravity is honest and direct, showing no pity for the fact that you fell down last time, and only rewarding behavior which works.

Unfortunately, as adults who have spent the better part of our lives proving to others that we are OK, it is often difficult to receive feedback about our behaviors because it is experienced as an invalidation of our ego, who we consider ourselves to be. And when the ego is threatened the reptilian brain goes into full attack/defense mode. We ignore the feedback, deflect it, and attack the feedback-giver by invalidating them. Then we get hurt and angry so no one wants to give us feedback for fear of hurting us or getting hurt themselves.

As you get more and more detached from your ego and practiced in the skill of eliciting and receiving feedback, you might be able to say, "Oh, do I understand correctly that what I did, didn't work for you? OK, let me see what I can do about correcting it. Thank you for the feedback." When you first try this you will experience the reaction of your reptilian brain and be struggling to not operate out of your old pattern of defense.

Later, with practice, you will recognize that receiving feedback is your quickest way to master your new skills and be able to actively solicit feedback with enthusiasm! However, don't expect enthusiasm for a while. Most people report the experience of receiving negative feedback at first as painful but necessary.

The other aspect in receiving feedback is that in most cases you are doing something different from what you used to do, but nonetheless it may still be dysfunctional (as in it doesn't work) and is most likely behavior from another pattern. This means that by receiving this feedback, you will be back at step one of these seven steps of transformation, *Recognition*, with regard to this new behavior and have an opportunity to clear up another pattern. It may seem endless, so don't despair, get good at transforming!

Here is an analogy. Most people beginning a new sport are, of course, very unskilled, which brings up many personal insecurities of inadequacy and being a failure. A good coach will only give positive, reinforcing feedback of what works (also a good parenting skill) which helps to encourage the novice athlete. If the athlete is given mostly negative, corrective feedback in the beginning then his/her motivation to do the practice will wane.

No one likes to do something when the expectation is, "I am going to fail." At the other end of the spectrum, the elite athlete will be asking the coach, "What am I doing wrong?" He/she knows that only by correcting poor technique or an inadequate training routine can he/she improve, and being already near the top, self-esteem is not so much an issue.

It is useful to manage yourself in the same skillful manner as the above coach. Give yourself positive feedback for what you are doing that is working, even if it is only one out of ten tries, and become more critical of what isn't working only as your confidence improves. In the process of practicing new behaviors, the likelihood of doing things that don't work and having to try something else is extremely high. You need to manage yourself to avoid the feelings of failure that are so easily triggered and to which you have been so long addicted. Only by maintaining reasonable energy and motivation for practicing the new behaviors can you sustain the effort and attention necessary to bring the new behaviors to a level where they become as automatic as the old.

EXERCISE 14

Your Conditioning

Clasp your hands together and notice which thumb is on top. Now unclasp them and re-clasp them so that the other thumb is on top and all the other fingers are correspondingly rearranged. How does it feel? Now take your hands apart and re-clasp them the new way.

Most people report that the new way feels strange, abnormal, out of balance, and generally not right. When asked to do it again, they note that it requires concentrated attention to get it right. Eventually, if you do the exercise enough, you will realize it requires less and less attention to do it and it will feel more and more normal. Perhaps after many thousands of times that might even become your normal way of clasping your hands—I have not run the experiment to see! The point here is that this very minor, often reinforced behavior pattern takes energy, focused attention, and intention to change. Imagine what it is going to feel like and what it will require to change a behavior pattern that is so much more of who you consider your self to be.

It is in this sixth step that it is so important to spend time and hang out around people who are either models of who you want to be or are at least supportive of your process in learning and practicing the new behaviors. They themselves might be working on similar life skills or at least understand what you are going through as you practice on them. The hardest environment in which to initiate new behaviors is the old circumstance, surrounded by old friends who have a vested interest in you being the way you were. It is like an alcoholic who has seen the light and dedicated himself to not drink, having to return to his old job as a bartender. It doesn't mean that it is impossible, just that it takes lots of extra effort and some very good boundaries with people as you assert your right to be different from the way you were.

In the eastern tradition people making these changes in their lives are encouraged to participate in *satsang*, which loosely means hanging out with an enlightened master and/or other people who are on the same path. That is not so easy here in the west, but if you can join others, even if only for an evening a week, it will help reinforce the progress you are making and re-inspire you to the required effort. Also having a friend or friends you can call who understand what you are going through is an important part of consciously structuring your support system around you.

Another important element of this sixth step is your daily sitting practice. In the quiet of your own space you will observe both the dysfunctional dynamics of the old and the promise of the new. Often I have observed that I wake up in a particular mood which, if allowed to continue, will trigger the old behaviors. By simply sitting with these feelings and thoughts and observing their nature I am able to let go of these potentially destructive tendencies. Then I can recommit to my new way of being and new behaviors and proceed with my day.

Another thing that I have found useful is placing little reminders around the house and office. Things that remind me to take a breath and feel my body and thereby drop into the moment with my observer turned on rather than sleep walking through life. In this way I am able to once again observe myself in action and choose how I want to show up in this moment—playing out the old or practicing the new.

7. MASTERY

"To be in the world but not of the world": to know you are the actor at the same time as being fully engaged in a role which produces your desired results. You are acting out of a script of your own choosing, so to speak. You are Being different, Doing different behaviors, and Having different results. You are conscious of what you are doing, yet it takes no effort to Be that way, as it is now the way you naturally are in that circumstance or situation.

I don't know what a fully enlightened master experiences as I am far from that experience myself, but it seems from my reading that it means being awake to yourself and in touch with who you are at all times. This awakeness is an enlightened master's natural state. This is not to say that we cannot be a master of who we are being at any time in any given circumstance. It may only require the recollection of the question, "Who do I intend Being in this moment?"

Once again the Eastern tradition has a nice analogy of this process of Declaration, Practice/Feedback and Mastery. The tale is told of the planting of the giant banyan tree. The banyan tree represents the fully developed experience of enlightenment, the master who is able to give succor to many, represented by its shade. While the tiny seed contains the essence of the fully grown tree, it can offer nothing and in fact must be nurtured and protected for it to survive and prosper. After planting the seed, its caretaker must water it, fertilize it, and protect it from the wind and sun. Even as a growing plant it still needs some protection and assistance. Many years later, it will protect and shelter its caretaker and many others.

You are the caretaker with the seed of enlightenment within and in this case, the germ of a new reality which is being declared into existence. At the moment of declaration, there is no evidence for this new reality and therefore no agreement or support from the outside. In fact some of your previous friends, who had a vested interest in your being the way you used to be, are like the wind and sun which would blow the sapling down or bake it to death.

You must seek support, a friendly environment, for the new reality as well as for your own growing mastery of the process of consciously creating your reality. As you get stronger and more centered in yourself as the conscious creative force from which your reality emanates, you will be able to withstand more and more lack of agreement around you. Eventually you too will be the banyan tree, giving shade to all who seek it.

As you complete more and more of the patterns in your life, in essence completing your past by extracting your Self from the various patterns that held you, you will find that there is less and less that you need to do to prove to yourself that you are OK, and you will be able to be happy regardless of what is occurring in your life. Isn't this what you have been striving for all your life? You have arrived, and experience a freedom and lightness of being behind the circumstances and situations in your life. Perhaps this is the heaven on earth we have been promised.

At this point there seems to be only one thing worth doing and that is to assist others in their quest for happiness. By having gone through your own transformation process, you certainly know a way (perhaps not their way) which you can share with them. However, simply being in the world in this new way will create space and possibility for others to make similar changes in their lives, so there is really nothing you **have** to do.

The Buddhists have a wonderful prayer "May all beings be happy, may all beings be free." This is both a prayer of gratefulness for what you have in your own life and your fondest wish for all others. May this book assist you in your attainment of all you desire.

CHAPTER SEVEN

Creating a Positive Reality

Your self-esteem is the foundation of the reality you are creating. Have you ever noticed that people who feel badly about themselves seem to continue to create negative realities around them? That old "Not OKness" raising its ugly head again! If that is what has been occurring in your life, you now know how to embrace your shadow self, using the *Seven Steps of Transformation* so as so create space for the new. How to establish a firm foundation of positive self-esteem upon which to base this new reality will be covered next.

As we are growing up, learning to be *at effect*, we establish the connection between our internal experience of being OK and the receiving of validation from others. Since we basically believe we are Not OK, this outside validation is never enough. This never enough quality of the outside validation puts us into competition with anyone else who might get validation from the same outside source. Sibling rivalry for attention and praise from parents is just one example. This continues throughout life as trying to get approval from others, looking good and fitting in, seeking validation through sex, and various other forms of outside validation-seeking behaviors.

Eventually, as it becomes obvious that the outside source's validation can't fill the internal emptiness, the outside source itself gets invalidated as in a teen's angry break with his/her father or in couples splitting up. This does not mean that the pattern is broken, only that you have turned to other outside sources like making a lot of money or having more and more stuff. To break this pattern you will need to observe how your own neediness (Not OKness) is driving your validation-seeking addictions. However, since we probably won't get to all the Not OKness for awhile, it is good to know how to establish a firm foundation in the meantime for your intended positive reality.

Creating an internally generated experience of positive self-esteem is done by establishing a set of operating principles for your life and then daily measuring your behaviors against those principles. The principles can come out of your self-determined core values such as love (I am a loving person) or generosity (I am generous with myself and others) or any other operating principles, which would determine who you want to BE in life. These are the principles that make up your character.

EXERCISE 15

My Foundation Principles
(20 minutes)

In your notebook, create a page labeled "Foundation Principles of my Character." List the principles which you are committed to operating out of and which will define the character you are choosing to be.

It is important to write the principles down and to daily rate yourself against them, remembering not to beat yourself up (feeling guilty and acting out the bad bear!) when you fall short, but rather practice acceptance and forgiveness of yourself. This review each day is important, as it will allow you to observe aspects of what happened that you didn't notice at the time and to mentally explore other possibilities of what you might have done and the possible outcomes that might have ensued. Be careful not to engage in "shoulding" on yourself: "I should have done this or that; bad me." By daily measuring your progress (I am assuming you are committed to Being who you say you want to Be) you cannot help but accomplish it. And making mistakes is a necessary part of learning—so get used to it!

Keeping a journal of what you intend, your vision and who you want to be within it, as well as your experience of the journey in getting there, is a very helpful tool. Often as you become more and more of who you want to be and have more of what you want to have, it is easy to forget what it was like back at the beginning. Your journal helps you acknowledge your own progress, besides being a place where you practice telling the truth to yourself. It will also reinforce your internally generated experience of self-esteem—the foundation for your reality.

ADDICTED TO BEING "NOT OK": BRIAN'S STORY

Brian had recently separated from his partner (she had left him) and he was feeling quite devastated when he first took the workshop introducing this material. After six months of observing his own behaviors, he realized he was addicted to the feelings of loneliness, sadness and confusion. He had had several opportunities to get into another relationship, but in each instance he had chosen to not go forward as he knew he still had work to do on himself. By not jumping into another relationship, Brian was stopping the survival mind's frantic attempt to avoid dealing with these uncomfortable feelings—to solve the problem, so to speak, by getting into another relationship.

Instead, Brian committed himself to re-experiencing the feelings, thoughts, images from the past, and the decisions he made as a child, which were running all previous relationships, and the reason they never worked. In fact, when a relationship is driven by the avoidance of the feelings of abandonment or loneliness (the feelings accompanying the Not OKness) then even when you feel OK and loved, the Not OKness is just around the corner because it is all part of the same pattern. Being in the middle of withdrawal from the addiction is not comfortable and it is easy to feel like you are going backwards instead of dissolving the pattern's hold on you as experiences and feelings long suppressed by the avoidance behaviors become conscious.

All addictions have their high when you get the fix (drug, alcohol, sex, relationship, a win at gambling), the agitation is temporarily over and you feel a sigh of relief. But the down must follow and it is this down that you need to observe, to be with and do nothing about. This is the opportunity you have been waiting for, in order to go through the pattern consciously so that it will disappear and you can create something different in its place. The only way out is through. It may take a while as each of the pattern's many aspects and levels are revealed to you.

As Brian was getting in touch with his feelings of abandonment, he saw that he put his ex-partner on a pedestal (she was his future salvation if he could get her back). He also had feelings of jealousy that she was growing and progressing and leaving him behind so that he could never catch up, which once again left him feeling hopeless, sad, and alone.

This mind fantasy, which is part of the pattern and links back to his feelings of abandonment from early childhood, was only there so he could justify feeling Not OK once again. As Brian saw these and other instances at home and work where he would set himself up to fail and then feel badly about it, it became clearer and clearer just how pervasive this pattern was and how addicted he was to it.

STOPPING ADDICTIONS

Here is a simple example: to stop smoking all you need to do is stop putting cigarettes in your mouth and lighting them. You must stop the behavior. This initiates the process of examining what the smoking behavior has been covering up. While it is uncomfortable, it is the most direct way of dealing with the addiction and has the greatest chance of not simply transferring the addiction to some new covering-up behavior. This is why the tool of turning your Watcher on and being able to observe is so critical. Only the light of consciousness can "disappear" the experiences that the behavior of smoking has been covering up and thus eliminate the need or compulsion to smoke.

Smoking is a good analogy and an example of our almost universal addiction to feeling Not OK in that so many situations in the life of a smoker will trigger the same smoking response: being bored, feeling a little uncomfortable at a party, or stressed at work. And if you continue to smoke while thinking you want to quit but can't, that too reinforces feeling Not OK about yourself!

THE DYNAMICS OF SUFFERING

The Buddha said that all suffering is a function of attachment—a grasping for what isn't and an aversion to what is. So suffering always has some form of resistance to the present moment. While no one likes pain, it has often been said that pain is just pain; what makes it suffering is what you add on top of the pain through your resistance. From experience I know that if you can let the pain be, without resisting it, it will let you be; and if you can truly observe it, it will disappear.

So suffering is a function of resisting the present and wanting something that doesn't exist. What we are resisting in the present and therefore suffering over takes the form of feeling abandoned, sad, angry, resentful, lost, hopeless, depressed, resigned and each of their accompanying body sensations. These are all the old familiar experiences from the incident(s) within which we decided we were Not OK. Often, I notice people keep some fantasy in place (a future salvation or a past regret) in order to justify feeling bad. This is a clear indication of being addicted to feeling Not OK.

Chuck's Addiction

Chuck was 53 years old when he related the following. As a young man he had attended a good university, where he was a star baseball player. During one of his first years at university, he had been offered an opportunity to play professional baseball. His father had persuaded him not to give up his good education, and later some injury had ruined his chances to play professional ball after university. Chuck was not happy in his current life and harbored feelings of sadness and regret that he had not taken the glamorous pro-baseball choice.

This 35-year fantasy of the road not taken was used in his current life to justify his addiction to not being happy. In fact, he resented the present, was angry because the present was not making him happy, and in so doing was refusing to take responsibility for creating happiness now. What Chuck failed to realize is that had he taken the pro-baseball offer, he would have been the same person with all the same patterns creating an unhappy life in slightly different circumstances! Once he was able to observe what he had been up to and tell the truth about it, he was able to move on to being more responsible for creating his own happiness, regardless of the exterior circumstances.

Chapter Eight

Relationships as a Spiritual Adventure

Achieving The Experience of Expanded Freedom and Deepening Intimacy

Many books have been written on relationships and I am not intending to repeat what can be found elsewhere. I do believe, however, that the dysfunctional dynamics between people in a relationship can often be understood in relatively straightforward terms using the models previously described in this book.

Once you are able to recognize what is happening, the dysfunctional aspects in the relationship can be cleared up using the *Seven Steps of Transformation.* The second part of the chapter will present a list (not a definitive list!) of the elements I have found essential in relationships that achieve the experience of freedom and intimacy for both partners.

The wonderful experience of falling in love is certainly a gift from the gods. Waxed eloquent by poets throughout the ages, falling in love is a very real experience that most of us have had at least once in our lives. Its incredible draw is that it contains so many of the experiential feelings we have been seeking: merging with another; losing that sense of bounded aloneness and the accompanying fear; feeling accepted and unconditionally loved; feeling you have found someone with whom to share life; a heightened sense of awareness; things look brighter, and the world friendlier; willingness to do anything as long as it is with your lover; feelings of unbounded happiness and gratitude for being alive; feeling free and reckless; feeling that every cell in your body is alive.

This urge to merge is a very real driving force behind most relationships and harkens back to some distant memory of our experience of oneness with mother and God. For a time, we let go and move into the experience of truly being with another unreservedly. In and of itself, this is not a problem.

The problem arises when you assign the cause of this wonderful experience to having the other person in your life. This tendency to put your self *at effect* is so universal (in that it is the underpinnings of the conversation you were born into) that you don't even consider that there might be an alternative. Poems, songs, advertisements selling almost anything, even some "how to" relationship books all come from the basic premise that he/she is the source of this experience you are having, not you.

You are having the experience, but without him/her around, you wouldn't. You are *at effect*, a victim in your own reality and now need that person to experience love and happiness. This fundamental assumption (and the need it creates) becomes the sponsoring thought of your reality. This gives rise to most relationship problems and is why solutions that come out of this same reality cannot ultimately work.

The second problem is the tendency to fall in love with your own fantasy. Early in the relationship that special person has enough of the elements you are looking for that your own survival mind ignores many traits and behaviors. The survival mind also makes up things which were never there in the first place so as to fill in the gaps and maintain this fantasy multi-sensory image of what looks like your salvation. This is the reptilian brain working hard to keep an old pattern in place by projecting onto your partner an image of someone, either real or fanciful, (often an idealized parent) that you have learned to relate to while growing up.

You then become the child/teen (identification) playing out the aspects of your personality that seemed to work for you in your relationship with that parent—either the part which is proving you are OK, or the needy, whining part which got attention. When this process of projection/identification happens you don't even know you are in the middle of an upset, calling it falling in love. You have found what was lost: the experience of once again being connected, accepted, and nurtured.

Unfortunately, what can be found can also be lost. Since no experience can stay constant, the high must wane, but the survival mind does not see it that way and tries to hold onto the experience. Finally no amount of denial can make the high stay. Losing that experience of connection throws you right back into the core experience of being abandoned and not-nurtured with all the concomitant terror and rage out of which you decided you were Not OK. Since, in your mind, he/she was the source of the experience of being in love, he/she now gets blamed for these terrible feelings which are surfacing: the emptiness, the hurt, the anger, the depression, the confusion, the Not OKness.

It would, of course, be possible to stop what takes place next by simply admitting what is occurring and taking responsibility for your own experience, but this doesn't usually happen. The relationship now takes a turn for the worse as each person tries to manipulate the other into being what you thought he/she was when you had those wonderful in-love feelings. Most therapists call this the power struggle phase in which the form of the manipulation is to punish the other person in the hopes that, if you punish them enough, they will come around to your way of thinking.

The punishment ranges from being unhappy, to withholding affection (sorry, no sex tonight, I have a headache), to complaints, to emotional abuse like angry yelling, to actual beatings (to get you to love me). It is all a form of the same thing: you made me (caused me to) feel so hurt, miserable, abandoned and non-nurtured by what you did or how you are being that I am going to punish you until you change back into what I want, or how you were before all this took place.

Of course what really happened is that something you did reminded my survival mind of an earlier similar incident from my past in which all of these feelings were present and I decided I wasn't OK. Telling the truth, which would set the couple free, doesn't usually happen. Instead they try to solve the problem within the same *at effect* reality which caused the problem by speaking out their feelings, as if getting them off their chests ultimately solves anything, or by establishing other equally unworkable strategies for never having it happen again. At best this leads to less intimacy and certainly less freedom. The great compromise in order to be in a relationship!

Much of the dysfunctional dynamics of a relationship can be understood in the following basic terms. One, the assigning of the source of your experience outside yourself, thus creating the need to have that person in your life so as to have the experience you want. And two, the projection/identification process with its inherent "I love you—I hate you/hate myself" cycle in its many variations.

And three, that almost always you are attracted to people with the same neediness that you have. Some writers have gone so far as to say that the neediness is the magnet, in that the part of my personality that is proving I am OK is responding to your neediness, and the part of you proving you are OK is attracted to my neediness (my Not OKness). It becomes a perfect fit at a subconscious (we are not aware of it yet) level. I have found that intimate partners always mirror each other's deepest insecurities until this Not OKness is released.

Two additional dynamics play out from this point. The first is that each person tries to hide his/her Not OKness from the other, because if you really knew how Not OK I was, you would reject me and I couldn't withstand that rejection based on what I deep down believe is the truth of who I am. Exploring this dynamic a bit further: the more intimate and therefore vulnerable you become (what we all hunger for), the more the fear arises that your partner will find out you really aren't OK and reject you. Then you will be abandoned again. So in defense, you push your partner away or get him/her to reject you on the basis of some superficiality. This sets up a "come close, no go away" cycle in most relationships.

The second dynamic is when you think you are OK or you have handled this weakness and identify the problem as being with your partner who now needs to be fixed. So in the name of love you give your partner the message over and over again, "You are not OK" which reinforces what he/she already believes to be true but has spent a lifetime denying. Rather than being appreciated for helping (which isn't really helping at all but the ego's way of playing, "I'm better than you"), you get some form of fight, flight, freeze survival behavior from your partner along with a good dose of resentment.

LEARNING LESSONS THE HARD WAY

My own life exemplifies these dysfunctional dynamics. I fell in love with my second wife when I was thirty-one, living in Hawaii and leading the *est* Trainings held there. I had been with other women since my divorce from my first wife, but this was different. I was head over heels, couldn't eat, couldn't sleep, in love. It was a good start of such intensity that I was sure she was the one for me. Through the years we had many wonderful times together, raised three great children, enjoyed invigorating camping vacations and relaxing romantic weekends, and generally enjoyed all the elements of a relatively successful relationship.

There were some major dysfunctional aspects, which we struggled with over the years, and eventually these are what led to our final separation and divorce after 19 years. The dysfunctional aspects are what I will describe in the examples to follow, even though it presents an unbalanced recounting of my life with this wonderful woman.

My years with my second wife were a time of deep learning for me, although I must admit I was a very slow learner, because I held onto my trainer/teacher, "know it all" role which hid my Not OK, not-good-enough shadow side, even at home. She therefore had a very difficult time giving me feedback of any kind, as it felt like an invalidation to me (I wasn't OK with her) which meant to me that she didn't love me.

That feeling of being rejected, of losing the connection with her, was my most dreaded experience and something I would do almost anything to avoid. Now I can see how deeply insecure I actually was, but at the time I firmly believed the outside act of confidence that my students all seemed to admire. It was only at the end, when she finally said, "That's it" and I was triggered into the sad, hopeless feelings of being rejected, that I saw what had been running me all along. By then it was too late for us.

While growing up, the personality I put together to cover my deep sense of Not OKness (inadequate, not good enough and something missing in me) was to be an achiever and be the best. I tried to meet or exceed my mother's expectations, or what I assumed they were, and in this way I got the love and attention I craved. I was the hero, the knight in shining armor, and the world was a big adventure where I was proving my worth to my greatest admirer.

When my wife and I first got together, I think I impressed her with my role as the powerful trainer in front of the room full of people seeking what I had to offer. But over the years, as she grew up and wanted a real partner in her life, I was too insecure to make the changes and go to the depth of relationship that she wanted. My survival-oriented ego was just too threatened; also I didn't understand the dynamics of what was actually happening.

As I look back, I can see that what I did was project my mother onto my wife and then I would become (identification) a teenager/child. I would try to get her to give me the appreciation, love and attention I needed for my heroic deeds in work and play, just like my mother had done. Also I needed sex to confirm that I was OK in her eyes and that we were still connected.

Here is a typical example of the dysfunctional dynamic. It's Friday evening and we have some plans to go out. I'm late from work and she makes some comment to me about not calling to let her know I was coming home late. She was naturally feeling a little taken for granted and hurt and expressed her comment with some anger. I would take this as a criticism of me rather than feedback about my actions and start to feel panicked that she was disconnecting from me. I would then do whatever it took to woo her back, being romantic, communicating deeply, helping around the house, just about anything, so she would like me and we could make love that evening, get the connection back and I could feel OK again.

After a restful sleep, I usually felt so OK with myself and good about our relationship that I would go off to climb a mountain or kayak a river, returning home that next evening the battered hero and expecting to be appreciated and welcomed with open, loving arms. Instead I would get an angry wife complaining that I had deserted her with the children all day and how once again she felt betrayed. This last comment I could never understand until I realized that, thinking her feedback had gotten through to me, she had let down her guard to make love with me. Then the more connected and intimate the lovemaking, the more she would feel betrayed when I abandoned her the next day.

Neither of us was aware at the time that this whole unhappy scenario was driven by both of our feelings of abandonment and Not OKness. In my attempt at not revealing my own Not OKness, I would invalidate her feelings of hurt and anger and at the same time justify my own right to do something fun after working so hard (sacrificing myself) all week for her and the family.

I often played this righteous martyr until I finally realized I was doing it to punish the person I claimed I was sacrificing myself for! By laying this guilt trip on her, I deflected her feedback away from me and made her into the problem. Even if

I sometimes complied with her wishes, I would punish her with my unhappiness because I wasn't doing what I wanted to do! So it became a no-win situation for her.

> **Dynamic One:** Assigning the cause of your experience to some outside source. I desperately needed my wife's approval of me to feel OK.

> **Dynamic Two:** Projection/Identification. Whenever I was a little threatened, I would unknowingly project my mother onto my wife, become the teenager/child and then try to manipulate her into conforming to that role so I could get what I wanted. She would sense my neediness and push me away, not wanting to relate to a needy teen, and this would only exacerbate the whole pattern.

> **Dynamic Three:** Hiding your own Not OKness. By being unwilling to admit my feelings of fear that she would reject me if I said how Not OK I felt, I created a whole set of strategies and counter strategies which only added confusion and a smoke screen that blocked my coming to grips with the real dynamic that was running the drama.

What passes for love in many relationships is the high before the low in an addictive cycle. This "I love you, I hate you" can't be love as real love has no opposite. This is simply some form of need addiction in which partners agree to trade something to get what they need. It is how most relationships start, so rather than making it wrong, it is important to recognize it for what it is and transform it into what you really desire.

In order to stop any addiction, it is important to stop the behaviors that are covering over the feelings driving the addiction. Then apply the *Seven Steps of Transformation* to the feelings that arise. For this reason, one of the most important aspects of a functional relationship is the willingness to confront your fears and tell the truth as you experience it in the moment and from the responsible position of owning that experience. This breaks the cycle and stops the drama.

Other important elements are: to give up blaming your partner for how you feel and for what is occurring in your lives; to give up having to be right about your view of things; and finally, to be willing to accept your partner the way he/she is without trying to change him/her. This, along with telling the truth responsibly, will set the foundation in place for a relationship in which each person can evolve.

Your relationship can be set up as a supportive space to transform what is arising or has been triggered in each of you. Then your relationship can become the ashram within which each of you are able to process out the inevitable patterns that must arise and that block you from the experiences of freedom and connection. When the negative feelings surface, you will applaud them and lovingly create space for them, rather than resist them and try to solve the new problem, as you realize, "Here is another opportunity, another step toward my liberation from these chains of past conditioning."

So what are some of the things that establish a condition conducive to a functional relationship? There are many good books on relationships that I do not plan to replicate. Here are some of the things I have learned over the years.

Tell the truth of your experience

Regardless of how uncomfortable it may seem, if you can communicate what you are experiencing it will allow you to deal with it before it manifests into something more damaging to the relationship. If you can catch it in the early stages, when it is still just a thought or feeling inside you, then you will not have to deal with the reality, which would have arisen, from those thoughts and feelings.

Most people refrain from having these truthful conversations because they tell themselves they are afraid of hurting their loved one. I have always found it is my own fear of rejection and my own reluctance to admit that I am Not OK, which has been the real consideration. This is an area in which you can build trust in your ability to deal with your own programming and patterns in a relationship, by telling the truth and living more courageously and authentically.

For many years, I hid the fact that I often looked at other beautiful women. Not that I was planning to do anything about it, nor was I fantasizing about having a relationship with them. I was just somehow, out of my conditioning, drawn to their beauty. I also have an ideal woman's appearance lurking somewhere in the dark recesses of my mind. I thought that if I ever said anything about it, I would hurt my partner and it somehow meant I wasn't loyal, loving and trustworthy to her. If she found this out about me, there would be a big fight and she would reject me.

Finally after many years, I was in a relationship with a wonderful woman and I decided I would screw up my courage and tell her the truth about what was going on inside my head. I said I had some crazy ideal and was drawn to look at beautiful women and I wasn't looking for anything outside what we had. She was confident enough in herself to reply "I don't care how much you look at other women as long as you take it out on me!" This was a giant relief for me and, since I didn't have to now resist looking, the pattern seemed to diminish and was certainly never a problem between us. On occasion, we even looked together and of course that meant she got to tell me about all the good-looking men that caught her eye. For me this was a great example of the adage, "The truth shall set you free."

Actively listen to your partner

Active listening is the missing ingredient in communication. People rarely experience being listened to by a good listener, so there are few models of how to learn to be a good listener. Active listening means creating the experience for the speaker that you have fully gotten what he/she was attempting to communicate. You have recreated his/her experience as it is for him/her, not just the words, but the actual experience itself. This has nothing to do with whether you agree or disagree with their experience, which is an entirely separate issue. And if you find yourself figuring out whether you agree or not, or preparing your defense or rebuttal while they are talking, you are not listening.

Active listening entails slowing down the entire flow of the conversation as you, the listener, repeat back what has been said and ask questions to help you clarify what the speaker actually experiences. Once you have fully understood the other, then and only then do you say what you wanted to say. An example might go something like this:

She: "Landon, I really thought you were a jerk at the party last night."

Me: (I have to really be centered to respond this way! I notice my breath and feel my feet on the floor to get into the present moment and, with practice, have realized she is describing her experience of me which may have nothing to do with my experience of me and then again it just might!) "Oh, that's a pretty broad statement. Tell me all the ways you experience me as a jerk."

She: "Well, you were loud when we first came in and you didn't feel where the group was and you then went over to Harry and started ..."

Me: "Let me interrupt you for a moment and see if I got what you said so far. You experienced me coming into the party without any sensitivity to the group, and being loud and overbearing."

She: "Yes, and you threw your coat on the pile and didn't even help me with mine."

Me: "OK, I threw my coat on the pile and didn't help you with yours. How did you feel about that?"

She: "I was embarrassed to be with you at a party with my friends."

Me: "I get that you were embarrassed and maybe a little angry at me as well?"

She: "Yes, I guess the anger started there, but what you did next really made me mad."

Me: "Before you go on, have I gotten the first part?"

She: "Yes"

Me: "OK tell me about how you experienced me and Harry."

If I had immediately tried to defend myself, rather than listen, this could have escalated into a huge battle involving "you always" and "you never", further hurt feelings, and nothing really being resolved. Instead, by listening and getting all the information on the table, it was possible for this upset to become an opportunity to see things like: how my insecurity and fear around meeting her friends took me into my loud, overbearing pattern; or how I reminded her of her father who was always loud and used to embarrass her when she was with her friends. You never know where the current upset will lead you when you use it as an opportunity to free yourself of the pattern and experience more intimacy with your partner by sharing what you discover.

Stop blaming your partner for your negative feelings.

It is essential that you take 100% responsibility for your experience. No one can make you feel badly about yourself if you don't already feel badly about yourself. So rather than blame the other, use the experience as an opportunity to find out where the feelings really came from in your past.

Stop placing the burden of making you feel good onto your partner.

Often couples stop blaming their partners for negative feelings, but still expect the other to make them feel good. This is another trap of putting yourself in a victim position within your own reality and places an enormous burden on the other which, out of love for you, he/she is trying to fulfill. This also reinforces the game of "I'll trade you for this if you give me that." It is a lot more subtle than outright blame, but it is just the other side of the same victim coin.

Stop using sex as a tool for manipulation. Instead, set aside agreed upon times to make love.

Sex can be a very subtle or overt tool of manipulation, from turning away without saying anything, to "I have a headache", to separate schedules, or separate quarters. By making an appointment, you are saying to each other that making love is an important part of your relationship (important enough to get it on the calendar) and it is an agreement to take the possible manipulative aspects out of your relationship. This does not mean that you could not make love at another time when both of you are obviously up for it, but rather it means that each of you has the security that you will be spending intimate time together on a regular basis.

I recommend taking your clothes off and climbing into bed. Keep the lights on, your eyes open and be with each other and try to stay as sensitive as you can to the energy between you. In the space of this intimacy, whatever is blocking you from being with your partner in a fully relaxed and joyous way will be available for you to observe. So this is a time to keep your watcher on, not to go into some fantasy. As your practice deepens, you can create this time together as your most sacred moments of intimacy and letting go. A time which continually brings you back in touch with your love and respect for one another.

As I have become more at ease with myself and acknowledging of my insecurities and fears, I have become more present in my lovemaking. There have been times when I didn't even like my partner and we got in bed to keep our afternoon appointment! Often we might start making love and then just stop and talk as the energy would seem to fade. Then, as we revealed what was blocking our being with each other, the block would dissipate and the energy might return, in which case we would continue making love. Some days it was mostly talk, and only holding or touching, but I never experienced a time when we didn't end feeling better about each other, and sometimes we had even fallen in love again.

Don't go to sleep without at least verbalizing what is bothering you.

Indra Devi, a yoga teacher of mine, once shared with me something that she claimed was the key to her successful marriage. She said, "Have a candle in a special place and if either of you want to talk, light the candle. Make it a commitment that if you see the candle lit, you will set aside time as soon as possible to talk." My mother always said, "Never go to bed angry." Both of these great women were telling me the value of not letting things fester, but confronting them as soon as possible so that neither of you suffers unduly and whatever it is doesn't manifest into more of a mess.

Have separate checking accounts in addition to whatever joint accounts you may have established.

This is something I resisted in my marriage out of my own insecurity and fear that my wife would somehow grow independent and leave me, which she did! You get what you resist. Separate checking accounts reinforce our basic nature of being free spirits. This sounds trivial I am sure, but money, like sex, is a big issue in relationships and almost no two people have exactly the same relationship to money, given our different conditioning.

The sense of independence and freedom to buy what you want, even if the checking account only has a little in it, is important to relieve the pressure of always having to be together. This giving each other space to be independent and free is important, not only in a financial arena, but in other areas as well. To accomplish this well, you need to let go of your need for the other person. In the meantime, it can be an intention and that in itself will allow you to see where you are holding on too tightly.

Accept him/her just the way he/she is.
Give up trying to change your partner.

I started several relationships thinking I had it together and I would help my partner get her act together. I also got into relationships in which I was the one being fixed. This dynamic actually communicates the message, "You are Not OK" while dressing it up in terms of love. This says, "I'm so OK (in comparison to you) that I will help you, who are not so OK. Now you should love me more because I'm so great and you who are lacking really need me." As you might guess, the help is resented, and your partner who is getting the message "You are Not OK" goes into all his/her survival patterns, including pushing you away because you may now see them as being Not OK and reject them.

As part of our Not OKness many of us have the pattern of "not being good enough." From this one down position, it is easy to slide into the behavior of trying to fix ourselves in order to please our partner. After all, shouldn't I change myself if he/she wants me to out of my love for him/her? If you can change using the *Seven Steps of Transformation* and genuinely feel moved to do so and, as a result, experience yourself as more of who you want to be, great. If not, it can set up a dynamic in which your partner (the fixer) is constantly angry at your inability or slowness to change. This lack of change usually gets interpreted by your partner as an **unwillingness** to change, and that means "You don't love me enough because if you did you would change." Now the fixer has started in on his or her Not OK/ unlovable pattern and the two of you are deeply enmeshed in a dysfunctional drama!

Acceptance is what all of us want and it is the foundation for being happy together. To accept another you need to let go of judgments, which are nothing more than a fear-based survival strategy for keeping someone at a distance and for not letting them in.

Judgments, of course, come out of your conditioning and past experience and are different from discerning between one thing and another or from having preferences and standards for yourself. It is the righteousness that goes along with the judgments and your noticing that they distance you from other people that is the key to seeing these judgments for what they are. Happiness is a function of accepting what is. So extend that gift to your partner and be happy in return.

Realize you have to consciously create "being in love", which is different from "falling in love."

Falling in love is an *at effect* experience, no matter how wonderful. As you take more of an *at cause* stance for your reality, you will find that you have to give up waiting for love to happen, and be willing to create love happening. This to me means creating romantic times and places together, then being responsible for creating the experience. I might remind myself, "This is what romance is for me right now. It is not some fantasy or image from my past." And then I attempt to bring myself even more into this present moment by noticing the input of all my senses. In this moment, this is it, it doesn't get any better!

Recognize that love is an unreserved feeling of wanting the best for the other person without any attachment to the form of your relationship: the wish for their happiness regardless of whether they are with you or not.

Once you are able to be happy no matter what is happening in your life, then you no longer need a particular person or situation to make you happy. The freedom this state brings will allow you to determine what is best for you both based on what is appropriate—not based on need.

From the position of appropriateness, people have been able to work out many different forms of relationships that seem to serve them. It is only your ego holding onto some notion about how a relationship has to be, or your fear of abandonment and the need it drives, which prevents you from operating in this non-attached yet highly functional way. This is something I am working on as part of my commitment to be a loving person. Knowing what love is helps me let go of all that it is not.

CHAPTER NINE

Taking this Material into Business

The extension of the dynamics of relationships brings us to a discussion of groups. Most of us learned about groups during our early childhood in our family of origin and in school. No wonder so many commentators on the subject equate dysfunctional aspects within companies to dysfunctional family models of codependency or the dynamics of the playground at primary school. This is the time in life when the strategies for "proving I am OK" are determined and reinforced to become the patterns of the future.

People from these dysfunctional upbringings come together in a company to make up the human element in the business equation. And the conversation in which they live, made up of all their conditioned behaviors, attitudes, beliefs, limits, fears and prejudices when unexamined becomes the Corporate Culture. How to affect this "conversation" is one of the great challenges for any business leader. For it is obvious that employees with positive attitudes, thinking out of the box, seem to create at a higher quantity and quality than their disgruntled, limited compatriots. To make any shift, the individual people have to wake up to themselves. The more who are awake, the better, but twenty percent, or even fewer at the top, can swing the company to a new cultural dynamic.

In my years of working with Fortune 500 companies in the US, Europe and Asia, I would often ask participants in the workshops I was conducting where they saw the greatest potential for bottom line improvement. Invariably it had to do with all the people in the company shifting from an *at effect* (victim) stance to an *at cause* (responsible) stance. They would claim that 40 to 60 percent of the human energy walking in the door each day was wasted in back biting, blaming others, protecting your own ass, not listening, not collaborating, and not taking appropriate risks.

Until people wake up to themselves and get their Observer Self awake, there is little chance that the corporation will be other than a replay of dysfunctional family and early childhood patterns. Even if you only hire the people who have a high need to achieve as their success strategy, you get the dysfunctional aspects that go along with it. I have seen many senior executive meetings in which it is one large dysfunctional family, with a controlling dad and compliant or covertly resistant children.

The material of this book could be the basis of understanding that would allow each person in the company to realize his/her full potential as a human being, and use ever-increasing productivity within the company as a measuring stick of how well I/we are able to create reality. In this way the company could be an environment of support for spiritual growth, rather than something people feel they have to do to make money. And rather than being viewed by employees as taking away from my personal development, working within the company would be the equivalent to *satsang* (fellowship with like minded individuals) in the East.

Here is an outline of how I would go about the process of changing a corporate culture if I were in charge:

First, I would establish measurements for the desired future reality. What does the vision look like and how will we know when we get there? These measurements would not only define normal corporate goals, but also cultural standards and behavioral norms as well.

Second, I would identify all the existing problems that need to be resolved or dissolved to create space for the new reality. But I would not do anything about them at this stage.

Third, I would teach people the material of this book in company-wide training sessions. Besides the understandings and techniques presented, the outcomes of these sessions would be: **1)** a commitment to a set of cultural agreements of how we plan to operate with one another which become the foundation principles of the new culture, and

2) an individual plan for each person aligning his/ her personal growth objectives with the vision and objectives of the company.

Fourth, I would establish a support system of meeting facilitators, individual consultation sessions, and group meetings to ensure that our new corporate processes were maintained, corporate goals reported against, and people's individual goals met. This is the important follow-up work that is so often dropped when attempting to implement sustainable changes.

Fifth, I would work on the list from step two so that employees can experience how relatively easy it is to resolve/dissolve problems from an *at cause* attitude. This would validate the transformation, which has taken place in the workshops.

Sixth, I would promote how special it was to be working in this unique company environment and celebrate our group and individual successes.

Chapter Ten

Frequently Asked Questions

How do I deal with Boredom?

First, I think it is important to understand just what is going on when you are bored. Basically boredom is one of the mind's ways of resisting being in the present moment. Your mind will be telling you, "I have been here, done this, before," which may seem true but is never actually true. If you swim across a river and then swim back are you swimming across the same river, in the same water, or not? Life is like that, it is never the same. By glossing over what is actually happening with a generality we give ourselves the illusion of sameness.

The antidote to boredom is to bring yourself more into this present moment, looking deeper into the details of your surroundings and the life situation you are in, and noticing what is actually going on in your internal experience. It means taking the opportunity to see if you can see what it is you are actually resisting and where it comes from. Here too is an opportunity for liberation from some conditioned pattern from the past, if you are willing to be with it and not constantly do something to avoid being bored. Once you are no longer bored, then you could change what you are doing, for you will then be making a true choice and not operating in reaction to boredom.

I have spent a great deal of my life avoiding being bored. Recently, I found that underneath the boredom and the agitation that was on top of the boredom (I had to constantly be doing something to feel worthwhile) was a deep resistance to being in the moment-to-momentness of life. My body was filled with pain, my legs ached, my back and neck were sore. I felt trapped and constrained and all I wanted to do was escape these painful feelings when they surfaced.

In looking back, I could see that much of what I did to take me out of present time with plans, projects, or intoxicants, or seeking pleasurable feelings through surfing, skiing, rock climbing, or sex was to avoid these painful sensations. As I have been more willing to simply be with the sensations, to experience them and explore their origins, I have felt a new level of peace and freedom from having to do something all the time.

What about Worry?

Worry is an addiction to feeling Not OK. When you are worrying, your current experience is one of stress and suffering, while you say you are trying to avoid some outcome in the future. Worrying is not planning! It is just another escape from being in the moment under the guise that by worrying the future will somehow turn out better. If you tell the truth to yourself about worrying, you will recognize that you are giving up the real experience of life, NOW, for some future fantasy.

If you actually need to plan for something then get out pencil and paper, sit down and ask yourself, "What are all the things that could possibly happen and what will I do in each case?" When that exercise is over you should be able to let the future be in the future and let yourself be in the present.

If you still continue to worry, then you will know it is an addiction to feeling bad and missing life itself. This too now becomes an opportunity for liberation as you give up the future fantasy, experience the body sensations, fears, thoughts, decisions, and images from the past that comprise this pattern and let them all go.

If you stay awake to yourself, every circumstance provides an opportunity for clearing away the baggage from the past and taking the next step along your path toward total liberation.

What if the other person won't change?

It always seems as if the other person is the real problem. If only he/she would change! First, I think it is important to remember that the way people show up in your reality is a function of your perception and your being the way you are (or have been). This is especially difficult to see when you get so much agreement from others about the way he/she is. Again, taking the *at cause* point of view, there is some way you are being that is not only getting a pay-off out of collecting the agreement from others, but also out of causing the problem person to be the way he/she is.

Once you say that person is a particular way, then you have pretty much cast them in stone, rather than taking the point of view that, "They are showing up in my reality based on how I am being because we are in a dance together. and if I change they have to change."

People completing my workshops on this material often report that after the weekend their spouse and children had all changed. It was difficult for them to see the changes in themselves because we each operate from inside ourselves and are somewhat transparent to ourselves, rather than fully awake to ourselves. Often it is easier to judge how I am being in my reality by what is being reflected back.

Remember, each of us is creating our entire reality, not just this limited experience called "me" within the whole. So it is always one connected whole, within which your major leverage point is to change yourself. That is why, when you take a stand for something or get clear about a direction you are taking or a way you are committed to being, miracles seem to happen in the reality "out there."

Lucy, (from the example in the Discovery Process section of this book), wrote me the following, some months after the workshop, which demonstrates how this all works. "After the workshop, I was on a high for days…. I felt truly free for the first time in my life! I was happy and I was sleeping soundly, and

I felt truly in the NOW every moment! That alone was worth everything to me.

"But, then, an unusual—and totally unexpected—thing started to happen: my son started calling me more and more, our conversations were more intimate, non-threatening, and really loving. I mean we had always been loving to each other before, but there was something else there. I'm still not sure I can put my finger on what, exactly, I would call it. It culminated in my son making a very favorable comparison of the two of us—something he had never done before. He had always been critical of my "flamboyance", what he called my outrageousness or weirdness.

All of a sudden, one day about two weeks after the workshop, he compared our fashion styles and said, 'I always thought the way you threw something odd into the mix was a little "off the wall"—like those leopard heels with the elegant black suit. Now, I realize that I'm doing the same thing with these velvet slippers and no socks with my conservative suit. It's a matter of style, and I got that from you.' Well, I almost fell over—my son had never aligned himself with me in any way previous to this—at least, not since he was a small child.

"It may sound like a small example, but what I started to see was that—now that I wasn't worrying about him all the time anymore—there was a different dynamic in our conversations. There was a freedom for love to be expressed, for intelligent, equal conversation to occur, for respect and consideration to be expressed and felt—by both of us. Suddenly, I realized that all my worry (about him dying) had served to do was to hold him at arm's distance. At the same time, I'd smothered him with my worry and attempted control of his activities so that he wouldn't get hurt—I thought!

What I finally realized was that I was trying to control his life so that I didn't "get hurt". I was interpreting his imagined death as a threat to my own survival because, of course, how could I live without him? I now feel that I could live with the fact that in any given moment, my son is either alive or not, and there's nothing I can do about that except love him no matter what. And, frankly, death would not affect my love for him at all—that Love, I know, is eternal.

"Our relationship gets more and more rich every day... And because I am free of my worry, I also have a lot more time to spend thinking about ways I can be productive and successful. I am opened up to life as I never have been before! I feel as if I have gotten my own life back—a part of me that I never even knew I had—with the added bonus of an even more special relationship with my son!

"Every now and then, I still get a tightness in my throat—while watching a movie where a child dies, or something awful happens at work... and my hand goes to my throat. But, now I know the trigger, I take a deep breath and say 'I'm OK, I am safe, my son is safe, and I am happy,' and the feelings pass."

Being with "The way it is."

In 1980 I was at the end of my tenure as a trainer with est. I was completely burned out in my job. This happened for reasons which I much later discovered were a function of my being the great know-it-all trainer, martyring myself to do the work and not acknowledging that I was an equal learner with the participants of the workshops. The balance of give and receive, teach and learn was missing—but that understanding took many years in coming.

By the end of 1979, I could not stand to hear one more person's problems. I was at one level an empty shell and at another level a man filled with a kind of self-righteous rage about saving the world. About this time, I heard about the Iditarod Dog Sled Race from a 76-year-old man named Norman Vaughan. Norman invited me to do the Iditarod and I felt it was about all I was up to, lots of open space and just being with dogs, not people.

The months of January and February, which I spent in Alaska, were months of intense preparation and training for the March race. I had never even driven a dog sled before January 1980 and I was going to have to drive dogs 1100 miles from Anchorage to Nome by myself over some of the most forbidding territory on the planet—crossing three mountain ranges, traveling along frozen rivers and even crossing a frozen bay of the Bering Sea. I had a number of people who had volunteered to assist me and more who had contributed to the venture as I was racing under an 'End World Hunger' banner.

As race day drew nearer, my competitive juices flowed faster and I even had some fantasies of finishing well up in the order of 60+ mushers who were starting that year. By the time I actually got to the start line, I was a mess. I was short and angry with my assistants, bossy and arrogant, worried about the race, already tired and just completely out of present time. I was especially not admitting or being authentic about what was going on with me. When I look back at a photograph of me starting the Iditarod, I can hardly recognize myself for all the tension in my face.

In the course of the next two days, I had a dog die, returned 80 miles to try and comply with a rule I had misinterpreted, and was visited by a small plane on skis to tell me I had been disqualified. I was devastated. I was crying and seeking an explanation from the pilot, who was the messenger and who wouldn't even look at me. I decided to go on anyway and completed the race in 21 days (under protest) in a year when nearly half the field dropped out. It is easy for me to see now that the trials and tribulations of those first few days were a karmic consequence of me being so inauthentic and out of present time.

It was after I had been beaten down by the circumstances and finally exhausted by the grueling nature of the ordeal that I finally was able to drop into the moment and simply be with the way that it was. I am embarrassed to admit that it took all of that to give me the experience and beauty of simply being in the NOW—especially since I had been teaching people that THIS IS IT for seven years!

One day about half way through the race, by which time I had caught up to Norman Vaughan, I took off early from our overnight camp near some trapper's hut. It was a bright, crisp morning after a new snow had fallen the night before. I followed the trail and my dogs ran along, seeming to enjoy themselves. As I came upon a snowy clearing, I was suddenly struck by the incredible beauty all around me. The air was absolutely clear, and the sun reflected off every snowflake, so that I felt I was totally surrounded by light.

It came to me that I was in my dream, living out the very moment I had anticipated and looked forward to in all those weeks and months of planning. Suddenly I was in the moment in the future when it was all supposed to work out; this was what it looked like when it worked out. Tears of joy and gratitude overcame me and along with them, a certain sadness over how much of my life I had missed because I was not present, especially with my wife and children.

I have never forgotten that moment and often use it as a reference to bring me into the present. Of course, I am always in the way it is. But often I need to let go of my expectations of how it is 'supposed' to be. Only then do I find that the way that it is, is so much more real and vibrant than any fantasy or imagined future could ever be. For me, when I open my eyes to this moment, the detail, richness, and beauty of NOW makes the fantasy but a pale shadow holding a never-fulfilled, illusory promise of satisfaction.

This, what has become a commitment to surrendering to the way it is, has greatly enhanced every aspect of my life, both in terms of my ability to deal with what is actually occurring as well as my experience of enjoyment. It has allowed me to let go of anger, which is almost entirely a function of wishing the way it is were different. And it has increasingly allowed me to experience a life that is both authentic and real.

I have the same patterns coming up over and over; how do I deal with them?

The first thing is to not get discouraged, as it is a long road to full freedom from our conditioning. One measure of your progress would be how soon you caught yourself as the pattern arose and how soon you were then able to ask yourself the question, "Who am I being right now?" Another measure would be how able you are to simply be present with what is occurring and not let it get to you: to maintain a peaceful, aware presence in the face of whatever is occurring.

When you first awaken to your own nature, you will start to see the patterns in their grossest, most physical form. By recalling your own history of the patterns playing out in your own life, your life experience will validate the models we have been talking about. As you become more familiar with your own patterns of proving you are OK to cover over having decided you are Not OK, then you will start to see the patterns for what they are—your ego's struggle for survival played out in an endless, unsatisfying, illusory game. And if you can be with that realization and let it be, then you are awake to this moment of Now, and to the real choices at hand.

I think that we start out dealing with our lives at the grossest level, the physical manifestation, which allows us to fully experience the ups and downs of life. And it is through these experiences that we define what we want and who we want to be. As we progress, becoming more awake to ourselves at a more and more subtle level, we are able to stop the automatic acting out of any given pattern and make choices which affect first the outside, physical nature of our lives and later our entire experience.

A metaphor would be a drunk walking down the road. He first staggers way off to the right before realizing in a muddled sort of way that he is off course from where he wants to go, so he changes direction and staggers way off to the left before realizing he has over-corrected. He then proceeds to overcorrect to the right again, but this time it is not quite so far as the effects of the alcohol are starting to wear off. Then again over-correcting to the left, and again not quite as much before realizing "I'm off track." This gradual awakening and correcting is the process of finding the balance, the middle path, through ever more subtle corrections. I doubt whether we humans will ever not have to attend to this corrective process.

An example: I was recently a participant in a meditation retreat that I have done yearly for several years, and by the eighth day of sitting was fairly attuned to my internal experience of body sensations, feelings and thoughts. As I sat hour after hour, I was having a lot of resistance to being there in the form of pains in my body and thoughts like "this isn't for me, I'm not really a meditator, this is a waste of time", and so forth.

As I started to feel worse and worse about myself because of all the pain and not having a very "successful" meditation, I noticed that in its struggle to defend some illusory image of MY GREATNESS my mind was not only making the meditation wrong but started to create a future fantasy of how MY work was going to save the world. This all took about 20 seconds! Seeing it for what it was, I was able to let it go and be neither disappointed with "how I was doing in the meditation" nor swept up and falsely excited by a fantasy future.

Here again was the same old pattern: one that I had acted out in years past, in which each aspect might have taken months or years. In the past when I started to feel Not OK I would avoid the situation. First I would justify my avoidance by invalidating the situation or other person. Then I would make decisions to change the circumstances or I would rush off on some wild scheme to make it rich or save the world. Doing these things, I only ended up reinforcing the pattern and contributing to my own eventual unhappiness. Finally, I was starting to see the pattern at its very roots, in the form in which it first arises. For this I am grateful and happy, rather than discouraged and disappointed.

Afterword

In my work with thousands of people, I have always been deeply moved by the grandeur of each one of us. Underneath the basket of negative programming exists a magnificent being of beaming love and compassion for others, of brilliant creativity and inspirational courage, of boundless peace and acceptance of all that is. This book has been about how to take the basket off the light that you are. So let your light shine. Oh! Let your light shine.

Workshops and Seminars

I conduct workshops and seminars throughout the world for the general public, teenagers, business executives and other special groups on request. To learn more about these programs and the current schedule please visit my website: www. LandonCarter.com.

Contacting the Author

I am happy to answer questions and am especially interested in hearing your stories of transformation using the material of this book. To contact me please send an email to Landon@landoncarter.co.nz.

Suggested Reading List

Rather than list all the books that have influenced me over the years and I am sure have contributed to some thought or other that I now can't remember, I will list some of the books I am currently recommending to people. If I haven't acknowledged some idea that you, some writer, lay claim to, I apologize and would be glad to include it in the next printing of this book.

Brad Blanton (1996). *Radical Honesty: How to transform your life by telling the truth.* New York: Dell Publishing.

David Brazier (1997). *The Feeling Buddha.* New York: Fromm International Publishing.

HH Dalai Lama and Howard Cutler (1998). *The Art of Happiness: A Handbook for Living.* Sydney, Australia: Hodder Book.

HH Dalai Lama (2001) An Open Heart: Practicing Compassion in Everyday Life, New York, Little, Brown and Co.

David Deida (1995). *Intimate Communion: Awakening Your Sexual Essence.* Deerfield Beach, Florida: Health Communications, Inc.

Paul Ferrini (1994). *Love Without Conditions: Reflections of the Christ Mind.* USA: Heartways Press.

Joseph Goldstein (1993). *Insight Meditation: The Practice of Freedom.* Boston: Shambhala Publications, Inc.

Gay and Kathlyn Hendricks (1990). *Conscious Loving.* New York: Bantam Books.

Gay and Kathlyn Hendricks (1997). *The Conscious Heart.* New York: Bantam Books

Harville Hendrix (1988). *Getting The Love You Want.* New York: Harper Perennial.

Esther and Jerry Hicks (2004). *Ask and it is Given: Learning to Manifest your Desires.* Carlsbad, California: Hay House Inc.

Jack Kornfield (1993). *A Path With Heart.* New York: Bantam Books.

David Schnarch (1997). *Passionate Marriage.* New York: Henry Holt and Company, Inc.

Sogyal Rinpoche (1993). *The Tibetan Book of Living and Dying.* San Francisco: Harper Collins.

Eckhart Tolle (1999). *The Power of Now.* Novato, California: New World Library; also (2005) *A New Earth.* New York: Penguin Group.

Neale Donald Walsch (1995-2001). *Conversations with God, Books 1, 2, & 3.* Also *Friendship with God, and Communion with God.* New York: G. P. Putnam's Sons.

Paramahansa Yogananda (1946). *Autobiography of a Yogi.* London: Random House.

About Landon Carter

For over forty years, Landon Carter has dedicated his life to learning about and understanding how we create reality and to sharing those insights. A graduate of Andover, Yale and Harvard Business school, he has been a trainer with *est* (now Landmark Education) and several other human potential and business seminars.

Landon leads seminars and works with individuals and couples internationally. He lives with his wife, Diane Covington-Carter, in Nevada City, Northern California and Golden Bay, New Zealand.

For more information visit
www.LandonCarter.com

Email Landon at Landon@LandonCarter.com

Printed in Great Britain
by Amazon.co.uk, Ltd.,
Marston Gate.